mind the gap

ENVIRONMENTAL ARTS AND HUMANITIES SERIES

mind the

gap

The Education of a Nature Writer JOHN HAY

University of Nevada Press   Reno & Las Vegas

Environmental Arts and Humanities Series

Series Editors: Scott Slovic and Michael Cohen

University of Nevada Press, Reno, Nevada 89557 USA

Manufactured in the United States of America

Design by Carrie House

CIP data published at end of text

"Sonnet 1" from *And in the Human Heart* by Conrad Aiken

© 1940, 1968 by Conrad Aiken, reprinted by

permission of Brandt & Hochman Literary Agents, Inc.

The paper used in this book meets the requirements

of American National Standard for Information

Sciences—Permanence of Paper for Printed Library

Materials, ANSI Z.48-1984. Binding materials were

selected for strength and durability.

FIRST PRINTING

13 12 11 10 09 08 07 06 05 04

5 4 3 2 1

To my dear wife Kristi Putnam Hay.

I also owe undying thanks to my daughter-in-law Joanne Crerand Hay for her patient help in following the manuscript through to its conclusion.

contents

mind the gap

Origins

I SPENT MUCH OF MY CHILDHOOD IN A THREE-STORY brownstone house in Manhattan, only a few blocks away from Grand Central Station. My father was a curator of archaeology at the American Museum of Natural History, a huge edifice just off Central Park. The Central Park Zoo was where I made an acquaintance with animals behind bars. Monkeys, loud tropical birds penned in a dark aviary that smelled of their confinement, polar bears and tigers endlessly pacing up and down, back and forth—all were imports from outer worlds I never reached. In the entrance hall of the American Museum was the skeleton of the great dinosaur *Brontosaurus*, with an incredibly long neck, like a giant derrick. Children still ask "Is it real?" when confronted by stuffed, or "mounted," specimens of animal life.

They know the difference. Were we not all born into a realm of hidden life from which our parents try to protect us?

The great city, made of glass and concrete towers, expressing a civilization's endless need to reach and survive, lifted our eyes to the space, skyborne, between the towers. Somewhere out there were glaciers, forests, great tropical seas—a world ocean in which the earth itself, symbolized in Indian myth by the back of a turtle, was an island surrounded by unlimited waters.

The roaring, humming city was constantly crashing and rebuilding, as if we were all destined to break out and surpass our own achievements. Perhaps the dark soul of the city, if it had one, might be seen at any street corner, as the crowds walked by, endlessly talking money, with hope or fear in their eyes.

I never climbed a tree in Central Park. The trees that had been planted by the city along the street seemed, when I thought about it, to be miraculously growing out of asphalt and concrete. They were only stopping places for dogs to lift their legs. But when our family traveled north with the spring on a vacation from work or school, I was in their arms again. I could grow where they and the winds of time, chasing the great spaces of a continent, had no walls to stop them.

Farm and forest were not so remote from the city and its suburbs as to be out of reach. A great city, despite its institutions of art and learning, might foster the ideas that man was not a part of nature and that it was a man's prerogative to conquer space, in all its manifestations, but I began to think, after many years, that such abstract ideas could not turn back the wind or the tides that are beyond our control.

I began in ignorance and in my old age I am still there, at some uneasy point of departure, but I have learned that what I can really count on is never exclusively my own. One of my early childhood memories is of being taken by my grandparents, on my mother's side, to graduation day at my grandfather's old school. My grandparents, too, had a house in New York, which they occupied during the winter, but my grandfather's pride and deep sense of continuity came from the farm in Ipswich, Massachusetts, held in his family name for 300 years by the time I went to college. It was a place of wide open pastures and farm buildings of great age. I loved to follow the haying season out on the great pasture. The wagons were pulled by horses of splendid proportions. The simple motion of pitching hay onto a loaded wagon under the summer sun seemed to bless the land itself, and to watch an unsaddled horse frisking and galloping over an open field brought elation to my heart.

On graduation day, we left their large white house overlooking the farm and headed out in a slow-moving car (in those days my mother seldom drove over 35 mph). It was a fine day in June. When we reached the school, I do not remember going inside. We stood out under the shadow of the trees that lined the campus grounds. I slowly followed my grandparents as they talked cheerfully with other decorous New Englanders and their sons and daughters. I was too young to follow what they were saying, but this was a ceremonial day, and I saw it in a different fashion: I was at its center. The light of the sun filtered through the radiant young leaves of the great trees and held me in. I knew, with unconscious acceptance, that I was singled out by the sun, my perpetual lord and master.

"A boy," wrote William Wordsworth, "I loved the sun." My memory of that day is not confined to what the poet referred to as intimations of immortality. I have lived through many years of accidents and violence, wrong choices and confusion, but in the sun is that great consistency that can never be turned away.

I saw the sun's magical face at the bottom of a well of stone. When I walked the shores of the lake we summered by in New Hampshire, its shimmering path came straight to me from the mountain on the farther side. As I walked on, that path of light went with me. I knew nothing of the physical properties of light. It may be no magic, from a scientific perspective, that our eyes conduct the light as it walks the waters. But miracles, like the everlasting dawn, are not ours to theorize about. We are sent ahead by powers we can never turn back.

Education

WHAT I BEST REMEMBER OF MY SCHOOLING IN THE first two grades of elementary school in the city was having my ears pulled by a teacher whose name I have never forgotten. Miss Halpern, may you rest in peace. Aside from that, I was set to work filling in the outline of an apple with red crayon. The juicy flavor of the apple was left to our lost imaginations.

My teachers were clearly exasperated by my lack of attention. So was my mother, who often asked, "Why don't you concentrate?"—a question I was incapable of answering. I suppose it might have seemed to the adults, at home or at school, that good behavior meant attentiveness, the best way to suppress rebellious feelings. When the sweet golden spring air flooded into our street and we opened all the windows, I knew a wilder world of waters and forest trees lay ahead of me. I was still faced with problems of order, common to a society of manners and civility. In the semi-wild surroundings of New Hampshire, the call of propriety still held me back. The same seemed to be true of my parents, who were usually restrained and well mannered, seldom exuberant.

I was at that embryonic stage of development when I had only to accept what was being set before me, with or without explanation. "Don't touch," "Don't meddle where you are not wanted," and "What you don't know can't hurt you" were always ringing in my ears. As I grew older, I had the feeling that what held my parents back from freely expressing ideas or contesting them reflected an age they were determined to hang onto. The Great War, which had moved in during the early years of their marriage, was seldom mentioned, but I sensed its shadow in their minds.

Still, what my sister and I were being introduced to during the summertime, especially on Lake Sunapee, New Hampshire, was an entry into an America that was always open, no matter how much order or how many fences were in the way. It was not easy, in a well-protected household, to "stray off the reservation." But our immediate surroundings looked out on a lake that was eleven miles long, and we faced a mountain never hidden by development, with green hills beyond that seemed unexplored as far as my eyes could see. Space was not obligatory, it was a definition of freedom. I began to feel, as time went on and a new summer came into view, that I did not know where revelation was waiting for me.

Lightning and thunder cracked and roared periodically as summer storms sent small waves rushing down from one end of the lake to the other. Wind shook the trees, bending them like so many instruments, and then subsided after sheets of rain. That world was bound to break into something new and unexpected at any time during the spring and summer and on into early fall. It was my teacher, even when I was only partly aware of its unseen depths.

Tons of granite were being blasted out of the ground to make way for immaculate lawns and walled gardens. This was accomplished because we were a family of inherited means, quite the opposite of the small hill farmers whose cellar holes could be seen in the hills behind us. We had a farm down the road with a small herd of Ayrshire cows housed in a stone barn and an adjacent dairy of frothy milk and thick cream. Not an extensive farm, but one that helped give me a sense of proportion, offering an equalizing effect, a closer, older accommodation to the lands. Across the road from the barn was a hillside pasture cropped by Angora goats whose wool was sent to textile mills in Massachusetts.

My father was busy planning a garden on a wide slope below our house that descended toward the shores of the lake. This "garden of granite," as he termed it in an article he wrote, required more rock moving and placing, helped by men of Italian ancestry who had learned the art of rocks and masonry in their homeland. It was these people, and the men who worked the farm, who told me what was missing in my life, such as shooting frogs in the marsh or using lamp lights to attract them by night on Chalk Pond, sawing down big trees for a view of the lake, and milking cows. (The frog legs, I found out, were unwelcome in our kitchen.) A summer's ice supply, by the way, was sawed into great blocks and came from the lake during the winter when the ice was thick enough to support a horse and wagon. The ice was put into the shed and insulated with sawdust so that it lasted all summer.

I had a little flock of leghorns whose eggs added to the supply at the house. After that I raised pigeons, whose squabs I sold, at fifty cents a pound, to my parents. When I was away at school, they were taken care of by a quiet and friendly man by the name of Steve Starkey, of Polish descent. Not until many years later, when I was in an army camp, did I make friends quite so easily.

We had no radio in our house for many years, and TV had not been invented. The constant reading of books filled my world with vicarious adventures. I had Daniel Boone and Robinson Crusoe for company. I joined Robin Hood and his men in Sherwood Forest, and I was with Tom Sawyer and Huckleberry Finn out under the stars on their raft, floating free on the great river.

I was almost enclosed by books, which became more vital to me than what I faced in school with its repetitive routine. Up in still-untamed New Hampshire during the summer months, after I had learned enough carpentry to know how, I built a houseboat modeled after a design in *The American Boy's Handybook*. It was a flat-bottomed boat with flared bow and stern. The *Blue Streak*, as I called it, moved slowly, powered by a secondhand Johnson outboard, but took me far and wide, way past the garden wall, out into all the inlets and tributaries of the eleven-mile-long lake. I carried a kerosene lamp for night travel. I fished for black bass. When I look back, I marvel at the space that was then free and open to me. I think of the lights in the cottages that lined the shores of the lake as magic lanterns lighting the way across the seaways of my dreams.

I was very proud of that boat. I joined it whenever I could. One summer, my aunt sent me a young goat from the family farm in Ipswich, Massachusetts, and I would take him with me whenever I headed out for a ride on the water. He was not a water animal, but he seemed to enjoy our excursions. On the way down through the woods he jumped with abandon and skill from one rock to the next, like a mountain goat. Back at the main house, I had him tethered to a stake. On occasions when he broke away, I had to run and tackle him before he made a meal out of Mother's favorite hybrid tea roses. He was neutered after that and returned to the farm when I was in school. "All good things," my grandfather said, "must come to an end." But that little goat named Abel and I shared a wonderful freedom. I was at an age when, in spite of an orderly up-bringing, I could see miracles wherever I looked. With that yellow-eyed goat as a companion, I felt that there was a freedom that was not obligatory but always waiting in the nature of things.

My dog Peter, an Airedale of astonishing patience and intelligence, also took part in those voyages, undisturbed by the goat. When he grew old, a process I did not understand, he was given a lethal dose, a blunt practice that was common in the world of farms and livestock. I watched the whole business of his being "put to sleep" without much outward emotion at all, so far as I know. I could not understand dying. The well was far too deep.

There used to be a sundial on a white pedestal outside our house. It stood at the bottom of some wide stone steps leading down to a long flower bed that faced a yew hedge bordering a hayfield beyond. Sundials may have had some value as antiques, but they were seldom consulted. This one was probably French and had outlived its time. The idea that it might have more than ornamental value may have entered my mind, but I was never told how to read it. The sun itself was an unalterable part of my experience. But we were not sun worshippers; it was simply taken for granted. Still, the sundial symbolized a corner for memory and repose. After my parents died, it was stolen by some thieves of time from the city, with nothing more in their minds than a quick sale and ready cash. The past was nothing to stop for. Too many bridges had been blown up, and a time for silence seemed to be thrown away.

"Steady now," says the sun, as a great band of light begins to expand over the mountain wall, taking all the tides of distance unto itself. "I am the past and the future."

The Past
at Home

DURING MY EARLY YEARS I WAS GOVERNED BY AN annual and daily routine that might seem highly oppressive in today's more disengaged world: "Here today and gone tomorrow." Yet that age, with far more space available to it, also had room for imagination, which was indirectly encouraged. At an age when it might have seemed to the adults in my life that all I knew was what I had been told to know, I began to feel as if certain mysteries were being denied me.

I had very little education in nature or natural history. I began to learn the names of a few trees, fish, and birds, but I felt held back by a formality that did not seem to go much further than the surface of things. There seemed to be endless trails leading out from the immaculate lawn, countless holes and hiding places in the fields and woods beyond us, which I was not encouraged to explore. Perhaps I was not old enough to go further into it. Perhaps my parents, especially my mother, whose mission was to subdue the wild, did not find it appropriate. Still, I knew the mysteries were deep in the "don't touch" places that I was warned about.

I was not aware of my own growth, nor how outside events originated. They just happened, and I followed suit. I was given every assurance that what went on today would be repeated in the future. The tradition that had held my mother's farm together for 300 years (I was at that celebration in 1936) was bound to last. My grandfather Appleton adorned the staircase of the family's ample home in Ipswich with photographs of all the presidents of the United States, from Washington to Coolidge. He had managed to acquire their signatures as well. Under Theodore Roosevelt's photograph was a letter commending both parents for having brought up four sons to serve their country. Their surviving son, Francis Randall Appleton Jr., suggested that I might do something useful in the future, such as being a historian. The idea struck me as an extreme option. Who was I to take on such a burden?

I was playing games, all the same, that reflected the times for which I was not responsible. Upstairs in New York, I had lead soldiers dressed in olive-drab uniforms. With them was a little field artillery piece, with which I was able to mow down whole regiments. When in the country again, I dug a trench in the slope above Dad's rock garden. I could wait there for an attack or jump on command.

I learned while staying at the farm that a General Appleton had played a prominent part in the great swamp fight in 1676, when the British colonists rounded up the Wampanoag King Philip and his wife and children and killed them all. What provoked all that I had no idea. I was not proud of it, but I was a part of that history. And the Salem witchcraft trials, with the "hanging judge," had taken place not many miles away.

There was an annual spring pageant in town that involved whites painted like Indians on horseback attacking a covered wagon. The Appletons contributed the old Concord Coach for the occasion, wheeled out of the stable, a beautiful sight, with shining and polished wheels and yellow and black paint. I could hardly blame my mother for unfavorably comparing such family surroundings with the dark trees and unforgiving rocks of New Hampshire. But the wild and unbounded held me closer.

During World War I, when I was born, the population of the United States was only about ninety million, low enough to feed a growing appetite for still-unoccupied space. Americans were famous for their optimism, even in the face of hard times. Our grandfather John Hay had left the closed-in, dangerous, and primitive atmosphere of the frontier to be educated in the wider world of the East. After graduating from Brown, he returned to the Midwest with a cultural appetite that would last him a lifetime. Among his later friends, which included Henry Adams, John La Farge, William Dean Howells, and Samuel Clemens, the name of Clarence King also stands out. My father remembered him telling stories about "the winning of the West." He was the author of *Mountaineering in the Sierra Nevada*. A man of his times, he was a great conversationalist and much absorbed by European culture. For both my grandparents, he was a witty and charming friend until, in later years, he married a black woman from Brooklyn. That horrified my grandmother, a devout churchgoing Scottish Presbyterian. I suppose he was seldom seen again in their home, though John Hay kept bailing him out of ill-advised mining ventures in the West, where he died in 1901.

"Grandpa Hay," as my sister and I used to call him in his absence, was a poet, the author of the popular *Pike County Bal-*

lads as well as a great deal of conventional verse. He and John Nicolay were private secretaries for Abraham Lincoln in the White House during the Civil War. They were the coauthors, after that, of a biography of Lincoln. It comprised a staggering number of volumes, which never tempted me; I kept a polite distance from them.

As secretary of state under Theodore Roosevelt, he took part in the expansion of America, way out beyond the setting sun into the Pacific, when the Philippines were taken during the Spanish-American War. The poet Robinson Jeffers was to write some unforgettable words about this expansion as a "thickening to empire." "Shine, perishing republic."

Manifest Destiny was another way to put a moral stamp on an incurable impulse. We who came later and admired the country's great open spaces, with the Indians and the buffalo, began to have our doubts about King's romantic "winning" of the West. What we had been winning we were also losing, at an increasing pace.

At the age of nine, in the British fashion, I was sent to a boarding school for boys in the Massachusetts countryside. Schoolwork was not too hard, once I learned the routine. I enjoyed football because I could get lost in the scrimmage (thus avoiding a sense of responsibility). Dad would send me "aggies" (agates) when I asked him, so as to add to my prestige and skill at marbles. I was also sent boxes of fruit, and some candy, which I hid from my friends.

Aside from the messages from home, what was really memorable about my few years there was a class in birds. The local minister of the nearby church took a group of us out in the fields close to town. We were equipped with little paperback field guides that listed some of the best-known species. So I began to learn about detail and what it might lead to, like a bobolink nesting in the meadow, the color of a grackle's eyes, the beak of a swallow or a hawk. Someone was starting to lift a corner of the curtain for me.

Hanging on the walls of the long upstairs corridor of

our house in New Hampshire were a number of prints by John James Audubon. They had been acquired by my other grandfather, who had died in 1905, ten years before I was born. To my mother they were only decorative. After some years she had them removed. I did not protest, because I was too young to know better. Yet at least one of them, a print of the extinct Carolina parakeet, had found its way into the depths of my spirit. Taste and tradition could never defeat wilderness America. A gentle ghost (my father referred to him as "the kindest of men") had left those birds behind him as windows on a continent whose nature was richer than any of us could imagine. I sensed that the land was not new because it belonged to us alone. The birds, in their tangle of vines, bright berries, and leaves, led me into unfailing adventures.

I was half New England, which seemed to be hanging in as best it could, but the missing grandparent, who had originally lived on the frontier, gave me hope that I might be schooled in something more than propriety.

The long summer days passed by uneventfully. Our voices were seldom raised without some rebuke from our parents. Mealtimes were always quiet and orderly. Civilization was an honored guest, and its darker side was not often brought up. We all leaned on order, and it prevailed, though we had to endure some uneasy silences when our parents seemed to be unable to say what was on their minds for fear of disturbing the peace. Debating ideas seemed almost impossible. Still, as an adolescent, I felt that I was living in the most beautiful place in the world. Whatever else was happening in the outside world to crowd it out, or deny it, gradually I was being introduced to essentials of space that were still unknown, and that never closed down.

School | Days

AT THE AGE OF 14, I WAS SENT TO ANOTHER BOARDING school in Concord, where Lucky Lindy had landed. On arrival, I felt so homesick that I wrote home to my parents, who were still at Lake Sunapee, expressing my misery. Mother wasted no time. Almost by return mail a letter came for me with the suggestion that I find a copy of Emerson's essays and read the one on self-reliance. I obeyed her will, as I usually did, and was told where the book could be found. But it was too much for me. I found the great man's style and meaning too deep to unravel, and so I quit. It must have been a disappointment to her. One could never quite measure up in a society of uncompromising standards. Our mother was a strong one for the truth, though she often stopped an argument before it reached its logical conclusion. Dad was blessed with an education that she lacked, never having been to college, and she found ways to make up for it.

The headmaster, or rector, of the school had been a missionary in the Philippines. The idea of moral conquest was in the air. "Fight the good fight with all thy might." Self-reliance was taken for granted as an ideal, together with other, much-admired American qualities embraced by the business community, such as rugged individualism and individual initiative, to which morality often took a back seat.

As children of God, we were all the same treated liberally, and the message was not applied with a switch and a cane, as it once had been. The boys at our school were required to attend chapel once a day and twice on Sundays, when we wore white collars, starched and stiff. When it came to be my time to be confirmed in the Protestant Episcopal Church, I made an effort toward independence by telling the rector that I did not believe in it, on the grounds that confirmation was an empty ceremony, of little meaning. The rector told me, in kindly tones, that many people, much older and wiser than I, knew better. My penance was to take extra Bible lessons for a term. I did not find them too disagreeable. The sonorous, Elizabethan tones appealed to my ears, though I had a hard time with the Epistles of St. Paul. Religious doctrine was way over my head. Was I finally confirmed? Yes, I was, and I condemned myself for my cowardice, but something must have come of it. In my unknowing but questioning frame of mind, I began to wonder whether my education, both at home and school, was not leaving out some concept of the holy and immaculate which was independent of their teachings. Could the voice of a hermit thrush, note after note, pealing with the quality of a crystal rain out of the dark trees, not inherit a stature that was at least equal to our own? Which world did I really belong to?

During one summer vacation our family rented a villa on

the shores of the Bay of Biscay, in France. From there, we set off on a side excursion to the Pyrenees. On our way through steep-sided mountain valleys threaded with shallow streams, bordered by close-cropped grass, we stopped at the famous shrine of Lourdes, located at the base of the mountains. It was at this grotto that a young peasant girl by the name of Bernadette (Marie-Bernarde Soubirous) had a vision of the "vierge," the Virgin Mary, in 1858. So Our Lady of Lourdes became one of the principal shrines of Europe, visited by thousands of pilgrims, many of them seeking miraculous cures.

I have a vague memory of what was inside the dimly lit grotto—some lighted candles, probably, and a central altar with a painting of the Virgin and many recent offerings. As well-dressed Americans stepping out of a touring car, we did not stay there for very long. We were quiet and polite, but we could not be described as devout pilgrims. Still, the place made its mark on me. The bare approaches outside, walked on by thousands of the faithful, seemed at one with the open plazas of the great cathedrals, such as Chartres, which we had also visited that summer.

We drove away, passing through one dark and spare-looking town with stone buildings. There I saw a man on the street with almost no nose, destroyed by some affliction for which there was no cure, or perhaps he was the victim of inescapable poverty and could not afford medical treatment. I thought of him as one of a vast multitude of people who had survived plague, war, and famine for a thousand years. He was descended from all the saints, martyrs, and knights in armor I had read about in books of adventure, one of the people who had chipped away at the stone that built the great vaulted naves of the cathedrals. A cathedral was God's house, and He deserved one that approached His majesty. It seemed that the "common man," as we used the term in America, was also an artisan and a builder. The people were the real cornerstones of faith.

I wondered at first why so many of the French women wore black, until I was told that they were in mourning for close relatives who had died in the recent war. World War I was still only a historical event in my mind, but I now began to see and feel it, in the torn-up battlefields of France. I also began to feel the enormous weight of all humanity.

Back in school, I hardly knew what I believed in. If I were asked, "Do you believe in God and His Son, Jesus Christ?" I was likely to come out with some lame answer, just enough to keep myself out of trouble. Still, my aspirations, such as they were, came out of the unresolved, the unseen, everything I did not know and which had not been explained to me. I was in the clouds half the time, which must have explained why my classmates called me "Foggy John." I did not know how to explain myself. Perhaps to overcome that, I had rebellious and combative tendencies. I enjoyed wrestling and the quick attack and was often much relieved when my opponent turned out to be weaker than I thought he was.

I took my unresolved feelings with me when we left for home on the Christmas vacation. The stock market crash came in 1929. It affected our family to only a minor extent, but as more vacations came up during the following years, the results of the Great Depression were clear enough. The homeless and unemployed were standing in long lines, shuffling forward at the soup kitchens of New York. Some sold apples at the street corners, and others slept on winter nights in doorways or on cellar steps, covered with thin overcoats. The rich among us looked away so as not to catch the eyes of the poor and commit ourselves, but we too were victims of chance, like the bankers and stockbrokers who were jumping out of the windows.

I did not know the world in terms of struggle and defeat. At the same time, I had no expectation that our lives would be much different in the future than they were in the

present. Still, the "future wagon" was waiting outside—
"Everybody in, everybody out"—and could not be denied.

If there was something about the school that did not fit
my undeveloped ideas of what it seemed to lack, it was also
protective. It offered a slow and undemanding view of the
past. We were being exposed to classic lessons in tradition. I
had four years of Latin, German, and French. I did misera-
bly in math, but my teachers in English introduced us to
writing that took us beyond ourselves to the discoveries
of America and the New World, and they helped us to hang
on to the rigging when the literary ships went out to sea.
We were introduced to the Oregon Trail and the poetry of
Kipling. The boys skated on the New Hampshire ice in the
winter and were rowing in the spring. We also used our
weekends to take long walks in the undeveloped countryside. What lay ahead? Perhaps a good job on Wall Street or
in an acceptable publishing firm, but the world we were to
meet outside the gates was enough to turn any poor little
rich boy away from such comfortable expectations.

When I graduated I got a school prize for poetry. The
subject was clam diggers, digging in the sunset along the
shore. One teacher told me that its style reminded him of
the Greeks, which baffled me at first, but I was encouraged.
I was still out there with the sun, on home territory.

Every day I passed by plaques to the honored dead of the
last war on the chapel walls. Our history teacher suggested
that wars followed each other every twenty years and that
we might soon expect another, but I was not ready for it,
and I put it out of my mind.

Lindbergh's Space

IN THE YEAR 1927, WHEN I WAS APPROACHING MY twelfth birthday, my father drove me down to Concord, New Hampshire, from our home on Lake Sunapee. Charles A. Lindbergh, who had recently made his famous flight across the Atlantic, was in town and his plane, the *Spirit of St. Louis*, was housed in a hangar just outside the city limits. It was inconceivable that this little silver metal bird, piloted by a single man and open to the weather, could have survived 32 hours across the North Atlantic. We continued into Concord, where the "Lone Eagle" was appearing on the balcony of the Eagle Hotel. We joined the crowd outside. I had a Brownie box camera with me, intending to take his picture, but I was still too short to get a clear shot over the heads of the people in front of me, especially the women of the '20s in their tubular-shaped hats. I stood on tiptoe and pointed the camera in the direction of the balcony and snapped the shutter without much hope of a result. Later, when the film was developed, I was elated to see the tiny figure of everyone's hero on the balcony.

When Lindbergh landed at the airport of Le Bourget outside of Paris, he had to be rescued from a torrential, irrepressible crowd. From then on, the press seldom left him alone. He was the victim of his own achievement.

When the infant son of Anne Morrow Lindbergh and Charles was kidnapped, public attention rose to a frenzy. I was staying with my grandparents when the kidnapper was apprehended. My grandmother and her daughter Ruth reacted with such violence that it shocked me. I could hardly believe that such well-behaved, genteel ladies could be talking about hanging, boiling in oil, and burning at the stake, medieval practices that I had only read about in books. They were so unadventurous that I could not believe they were joining in an ancient chorus of accusers from which no one was immune.

Lindbergh shadowed my generation for many years. He was accused during World War II of sympathizing with the Nazis in Germany, especially during the years before the outbreak of the war. He was awarded by Hermann Goering for his interest in the Luftwaffe. But he sent back a great deal of information to the United States about the condition of the German air force, which seemed to take him out of that shadowy realm of sympathy with totalitarianism.

For a great many Americans rooted in the pioneering days, Lindbergh was a prototype of the self-reliant man, like Daniel Boone, who could not tolerate living within ten miles of a house, or Nattie Bumpo of James Fenimore Cooper's novel *The Prairie*. There was a streak of austerity in him, probably inherited from his Scandinavian ancestors, who believed in character steeled by adversity. Strong character, which my mother's people certainly believed in, implied stoicism, the endurance of pain. Something that hurt you was good for you, like alcohol on a wound. John Muir, the great naturalist, was semitrapped in a deep well he was digging on the family farm in Wisconsin. His Calvinist father, when called upon to rescue him, suggested that he had better learn to rescue himself. Lindbergh's father reacted in much the same way when his son fell out of a boat.

The self-made man was very much admired. It was not money but endurance that captivated the imagination of the young. I did my best to follow such examples, but I was always falling short.

Heroes and heroines were less subject to instant dismissal than they are in more cynical times. After his famous flight, Lindbergh was awarded the title of "Lucky Lindy," as if he had won the sweepstakes, or big money on Wall Street, awarded by a nation of instant gamblers.

Lindbergh became a lonely and controversial figure for many Americans, but he was always associated in my mind with his personal conquest of space, which meant a good deal more than mere claiming and occupation. He allied himself with it, as he must have done when he carried mail in his small plane over the sparse regions of the West. Wings, and the liberating sense of soaring high through the clouds like a bird, would not have been far from his mind.

Later in life, after he and his family had moved from the United States to the comparative seclusion of Hawaii, Lindbergh became a dedicated and influential conservationist. He lamented that there was little in America to hold on to anymore. He spoke of a lack of contact, using the image of the original broadax connecting with a tree in the wilderness. Conquest of the land and Manifest Destiny were losing not only the vision but the physical presence of a continent of unprecedented space. A sense of primal distance was being lost to sight.

Travel

TRAVEL, WHEN I WAS GROWING UP, NEVER SEEMED TO have lost its original ties to Europe. That is where most of us came from. There were those in this country who regretted losing the stabilizing influence of the British Empire when they felt the present state of the nation was being threatened with a lack of order and stability. Growing power sent America off on foreign adventures never recommended by George Washington. The land itself, as it was taught—or ignored—was treated as worthy of our attention only if it served our material ends. "Go West, young man" had expanded into Manifest Destiny, which only seemed to have resulted in land grabs, gold rushes, and feeding frenzies beyond the setting sun. Still the tugs toward Europe were strong yet, at least as I saw it in my parents. The truth is that, with the exception of my father, who made annual trips to Mexico for the American Museum, we never went farther than the eastern seaboard. The deserts and the mountains of the West were too difficult to reach, in spite of the pioneers. My grandmother regarded the sovereign state of Texas, for example, with abhorrence. Who could live in such an outlandish place? It was still much safer in the East.

The result was that my sister and I were taken, a number of times, to England and France. Italy, for reasons not explained, was left out of the itinerary so far as the children were concerned.

The family climbed up the gangplank of whatever cavernous ocean liner was docked along New York's East River, counting the luggage once again. We were following in the wake of hundreds of thousands of Americans backtracking across the Atlantic for a hundred years or more behind us. Some were on literary pilgrimages, visiting the birthplaces of famous authors. Others were hungry for the masterpieces of painting and sculpture. Many were attracted by the Eiffel Tower in Paris or Napoleon's Tomb. In London, they took in the changing of the guard outside Buckingham Palace or the gloomy Tower of London, where famous prisoners had awaited their execution.

Our parents were interested in gardens, public or private, which broke the routine. We drove through the English countryside, stopping at inns or estates, as if habituated to such comforting scenery. Both countries had their share of medieval castles, ruined monasteries, churches and cathedrals and, in France, the chateaux. The historic places provided some relief from the constant demands of a busy nation out to prove that the past was expendable, any day, any time or place, but I began to be tired of facades and acceptable scenery. After walking through a mile of galleries at the Louvre, only to see a portrait of Mona Lisa, I failed to understand why my parents were out to wreck my feet.

As a teenager, with a head full of romantic machinery

that often seemed useless in the world that was being pre-
sented to me, I felt alone, without knowing the reasons for
it. Perhaps I missed being out on my houseboat, floating at
its own slow pace under the stars, in a great new country
that was forever free. At the same time, I knew that the
earth's geography was full of strange and wonderful spaces
that were far away but real enough to fill my imagination
with confidence. These were to be seen at home, in the halls
of the American Museum. Its dioramas, ranging from the
South Seas to the polar regions, were like windows, open to
unending possibilities.

I saw timber wolves chasing deer across a snowy clearing
in the forest, and they pulled me in; I could scarcely be
torn away. The tiger brought down the antelope. The ele-
phant plodded slowly across the African savanna. Warm seas
poured in without interruption toward islands full of monkeys and birds on tropical vines. One familiar exhibit was of
our forest brook in New Hampshire that used to provide us
with the purest of waters. Its centerpiece was a great rock I
had passed by many times, which was being visited by a
blue jay and a foraging mink. These were not just "stuffed"
animals but alive, in the distances I yearned for.

Dad was a curator of archaeology in the Department of
Anthropology. As a boy, I met Roy Chapman Andrews there,
the discoverer of dinosaur bones in the Gobi Desert. George
Vaillant, who wrote a book on the Aztecs, was a good friend
of our father's. Margaret Mead was also in the department.
Many years later, I was to know Robert Cushman Murphy,
chairman of the Department of Ornithology and author of
The Oceanic Birds of South America. In a world of scholars who
did not stay too long within their own disciplines, his favorite reading was Dante's *The Divine Comedy*.

Dad did not rank high among his colleagues so far as his
work was concerned, though he discovered a small temple
in Yucatan called Temple B, at Rio Bec. My sister and I heard
very little about his experiences in Mexico. He was not

given to saying very much about himself. He was too lacking in self-confidence to make bold statements on his own behalf. As Alfred Marston Tozzer, of the Peabody Museum at Harvard, said of him, he was one of the great band of dirt archaeologists—especially in his younger days—who did not have the advantage of extravagant equipment.

He was a man of quiet wit and intelligence, charming his friends and associates with his plays on words, probably acquired from his father. The large rock garden he planned and installed at his home in the hills shows an imagination that understood landscapes as a whole—and there was love. As my sister said, "He loved every rock and tree in the place."

Each new plant had his painstaking attention. He left a box of filed cards that recorded 640 plantings. Each one listed the date and time, the location, soil condition and recommendation. He also listed each plant's success or failure. In 1999, I saw a single little blue flower growing under a narrow ledge that jutted out from a bank over the lower reaches of the rock garden. Its name was Rowanda, and the record showed that Dad had planted it there in September of 1936. Next to that entry was a note that said "OK." So that inconspicuous flower had survived 63 northern winters. That would have delighted the man who planted it where he thought it ought to be, precisely placed in its rock shelter.

We are dignified, not by the world's opinions but by the company we keep. Knowing him, I doubt that he would have made much of his success, though he could not have failed to be pleased by it. It was an experiment, and OK would do, after he saw it safely planted. Still, it seems to me that he and Rowanda have been on a deeper journey together than most of us could anticipate. Seeing into the grounds of space and time required the man and the flower together, not in isolation, one from the other.

The last time I remember going on a trip with my father and mother, perhaps in the summer of 1936, we were headed for the annual summer music festival in Salzburg, Austria, where the soprano Lotte Lehman was to sing in Richard Strauss's opera *Rosencavalier*. On the way, we stopped in Munich, Bavaria, where I saw a young man in a brown shirt crossing a square on a bicycle. He spotted a friend and greeted him with the raised arm of a Nazi salute.

From that trip two things stand out in my memory. One is Lotte Lehman's beautiful voice, the other is that salute. Something ominous was in the air. Was Europe to unravel once again? I was torn between admiration for a history so rich in tradition and art and an ominous feeling of threat. I did not know where I belonged. Unexpected walls were rising in front of me.

Climbing the Steps

IN THE YEAR 1934, I WAS SEATED AT A SMALL DESK along with many others in Harvard's Memorial Hall. It was during the week set aside for freshman orientation, and I was in a state of semiparalysis. It surprised me that I had been admitted to Harvard in the first place, because I thought I had done so badly on the college entrance exams. In that splendid high-ceilinged edifice, I had no idea of what was to come, or what was expected of me. That feeling lasted a long time while I tried to find my way through those hallowed halls. I was not up to it. I was a fish out of water. I was scared, just as I was scared of girls in those days, unlike, so I thought, so many of my braver and bolder classmates. If I saw a very pretty girl swinging down the street and I desperately wanted to know her, I had no idea of how to go about it.

Such vital tests of my infirmity as exams began to sneak up on me. I thought I would do well in Latin, since I had had so much of it in school. Geology attracted me because I thought it might take me outdoors, and so it did, if in a limited way. I was halted by its mathematics. Of course, the faults and the fractures were in myself as usual. "Mother dear, where is the strong character you hoped to see in me?"

I had consulted a tutorial bureau, which sold me "crib sheets" to help with my history exam, but that did not help very much. When the college year was over, I do not think I had a passing grade in much of anything. I spent much of the following summer taking remedial courses in summer school. And with the help of English lit—at least I was a good speller—I made my way back again.

While I had the feeling that the world outside was suspended between the economic depression and threats of war on the horizon, I took refuge in a fortress of words. In the beginning, of course, was the Word, and the Word came from God, but most of what I was subjected to seemed to come from Man, or as my father used to say, "Homo Sap." I concentrated in English lit from the Anglo-Saxon to the twentieth century and began, with varying degrees of success, to pass my examinations.

I began to move by fits and starts into the world of ideas, with little sense of where it might be taking me. The darkness of the Great War, which my college friend Howard Nemerov, the poet, later described as a smashup between the horse and the motorcar, had moved off like a storm, but the shell-shocked trenches lingered in my mind. At times, I suppose, I thought of human civilization as an overwhelming artifact prone to periods of decline and degradation. Unconsciously, I think, I did not want to be uprooted at that stage of my life. I had only dimly worked out that what I had thus far experienced of hope and freedom issued from the immortal nature of a land I had hardly begun to know.

For a while, I was attracted to the pragmatic philosophy of John Dewey, from self-reliant Vermont. I was also interested in the consumer cooperative movement, having read a book by Marquis W. Childs called *Sweden, the Middle Way*. I was afraid of extremes or of being forced into them. I sat in on some of the classes of the philosopher Alfred North Whitehead, author of *Science and the Modern World*, but without much science behind me, I was cast adrift by his advanced methods of thought.

I did not believe in Original Sin at the time, though later exposure to the twentieth century began to change my mind. Nor did I quite grasp the meaning of heaven and hell as I met them in school and college. They held a certain storybook fascination for me, but I could not defend what I did not grasp. I believe it was Karl Marx who said that religion was "the opiate of the masses." I was not carried away by such a thought, as I knew the people of any country deserved their faith and religious practices.

I was at that familiar stage of adolescence when we hardly know who we are and run, head-on, into confusion. Too many worlds were being introduced to me, and it was hard to choose between them. I felt threatened by circumstances for which I was not responsible. This is called "growing up." But one day, when I was sitting in a classroom or the library, doing nothing in particular, I was suddenly transformed by a feeling that I was going to live forever. It had nothing to do with my surroundings; I was being taken by a nameless joy. Daily rounds came back soon enough, but I felt as if my body knew more than my mind.

Guided through centuries of English lit, I was doing reasonably well with my grades. I was being practiced in a tradition that I had been exposed to in school and, to some extent, at home. I was none too sure of my ability to write or to improve my "attention span," but I was getting by. Passing grades were as important to success as they are today. But what of the future?

Most undergraduates in those days were not capable of answering such a question. We seemed to be half suspended between the present and the past, and the future was only problematical. We were at the stage when we might speak heatedly about Sigmund Freud and Carl Jung, without knowing very much about either of them. What we got out of it were useful phrases such as "split personality" or "inferiority complex," which we used to describe what was wrong with our friends.

The Spanish civil war came along, and I recall strong arguments with an artist classmate of mine, a Roman Catholic, while we shared meals in Lowell House. He was strongly in favor of General Franco, and I was a Loyalist, almost ready to volunteer, like some European and American writers of the day, to go over and fight for a democratic cause. Long-distance combat was in our minds, and chance events none of us could predict.

My college years strengthened my love of books and encouraged me to write. Aside from that, I had no great confidence in my own abilities. I had found no subject, though I was being introduced to them all the time. The language of poetry was international, and it did not matter whether I was reading John Donne or Emily Dickinson—a tone of mystery came through. But while I was concentrating on seventeenth- or eighteenth-century prose and poetry, I was also being confined to one tradition and its formalities. I did not know how to break away and speak in terms of my own country. I felt that I was being confined by history, and history was beginning to feel like a trap.

I never took a course in American writing or literature, to my great regret. We read a few of Walt Whitman's poems in school, but they were only samples of his work. "Song of

Myself" hit me, years later, like a fresh voice out of incomparable space. *Moby Dick* was also touched on at school, but I never felt its magnitude until much later on.

I accused myself of being too obedient, but I did not know how to break away. When I finally walked away from the college yard, world war was gathering its powers and starting to sweep all tradition and precedence away once again. I had no idea of what I was to do with my life. We were all being moved out of context, pulled from our roots, and delivered to the mercy of an age that only existed in terms of its own momentum.

The Poet

THE FIRST TIME I MET CONRAD AIKEN WAS AT HIS HOUSE in Rye, in Suffolk, England. After graduating from college, I was on my way, in the fall of 1938, to Geneva, where there was a slim possibility of getting a job at the International Labor Office. I had known its director, John Winant, when he was governor of New Hampshire and I was at St. Paul's School, and he had encouraged me.

A friend of mine at Harvard, a writer named Dunstan Thompson, was one of five or six students of varying ages at the Aikens' summer school. Mary Hoover Aiken taught drawing and painting, and Conrad Potter Aiken took on the writers, to read and discuss their manuscripts. Mary, as I was soon to find out, was also an exceptional cook, having learned Spanish cuisine when she was studying art in Spain.

They lived in Jeake's House, which stood by a cobblestone street leading toward the Romney Marshes in the distance and the sea beyond. Rye was one of the Cinque Ports, which included Hastings, of the Norman Conquest; it was a coast once filled with the traffic of sailing ships and watchful eyes.

The first words Conrad spoke to me when I was ushered in the door were, "Do you enjoy music?" "Well, I do," he said, breaking the silence while I was thinking of something to say. "I am particularly fond of Mozart."

My friend Dunstan walked out with me later on to a parapet behind the house, overlooking the marshes, and said, "What did you think?" He was one of the kind who likes quick assessments to chew on, but I had only been there for a few hours.

Other navigators of the arts had been attracted to Rye for many years. Joseph Conrad had lived in a large house in the town, and Henry James had moved from London in the latter part of his life to a smaller house not far from Jeake's House. While I was there, the painter Ed Burra came for a visit and he and Conrad repaired to the nearby Mermaid's Tavern. The Aikens often visited the pub to enjoy a drink or two with the proprietor, Tiny Morton.

T. S. Eliot, a classmate of Conrad's, lived in London at the time. Although they were friends, Conrad was clearly bothered by the attention that was being given to The Wasteland, while his own writing was being left in the shadows.

I met Robert Flaherty, the early filmmaker, famous for Nanook of the North, at Jeake's House, and there was Dame Laura Knight, who lived some distance away but had often used a local one-ring circus as the subject of her paintings. I must have been in Rye for only the better part of a week, but during that time the little circus arrived. It spread out its tent over open ground on a lower level of the town, and I have never enjoyed anything quite so much. It was a miniature version of Barnum and Bailey, but its appetite surpassed its size. Held in balance under the one tent were several trapeze artists on the high wire. Clowns and acrobats would period-ically dash into the tent to the sound of applause, and a single rider performed stunts from the back of a white horse prancing around the ring. Pigeons, at the sound of a gunshot from a small cannon, would suddenly burst into the air like a bunch of flowers.

I remember making comparisons at the time with the Bradford and Newbury Fair in New Hampshire, which we used to visit every year. The animals in their pens were not overwhelmed by their numbers. The suckling pigs, the goats, and the sheep stood out in their singularity. I remem-ber the fantail pigeons, like little white carvings, and the game cocks and the bantam hens and the roosters, for their alertness and colors. The patient ox and the great farm horse held the center at the weight-pulling contests while the roosters crowed. The small farms had an art of their own, bred of familiarity and affection, like the farmboy in his enclosure guarding a lamb.

The following year, I found a job in Washington, D.C., as correspondent for the Charleston (S.C.) *News and Courier*. It was low paid and not too exacting, but I enjoyed my con-nection with the South, visiting Charleston several times. By modern standards the nation's capital, especially during the summer, was hot and muggy, and it still had some of the characteristics of a quiet southern town. I interviewed sena-tors and congressmen and began to grasp some of the ma-chinery of government. Some minor news was always avail-able to keep the people of Charleston up-to-date. In the time I spent there, nearly two years, I only managed one headline in the newspaper, when a committee chairman, a Carolin-ian, accused someone at a committee meeting of having communist sympathies.

During that period, I met Kristi Putnam, my future wife. She was the daughter of George Putnam, who had been the U.S. Commissioner of Lighthouses. Our marriage, at least, turned out to be permanent.

It must have seemed to me, all the same, that I was only marking time. The world had other plans for me. Though jobs were important in order to prove one's reliability in society, my own unformed ambitions were being passed by. What I wanted to do was write, with nothing else in mind. Where was I to find a true subject in myself while being constantly dislodged?

War broke out in Europe in 1940, and my feelings were reflected in the minds of millions. When it became clear that the United States was to join its allies against Hitler's Germany and that I would be called up for service, I thought of the Aikens. I saw Conrad Aiken as offering me a chance, however brief, to learn more of the art of writing from a master. I had never met such a man. As I saw it, my education had been lacking in teachers who were true practitioners of creation, who on their own were committed to following wherever the spirit led them. I saw freedom in the Aikens of a kind I yearned for. They were mystifying to me at first, but it was clear that they were deeply dedicated to the life they shared, come what may. They had abandoned Jeake's House and found an old farmhouse in Brewster, on Cape Cod. So I wrote them and they agreed to take me on as a student paying room and board.

The farmhouse they'd moved into was long and low, covered with the typical wood shingles. They had named it Forty-One Doors. On the first day, they drove me out in their Model T Ford to pay a visit to Edwin Duckinson and his wife in Wellfleet. The car was called Libido, a name honoring the gods of love and sex. It was a somewhat dilapidated little vehicle, painted a light gray, with torn curtains hanging from its windows, indicating their sense of a comforting poverty. Conrad had written from England, informing me that they were so poor that they had to sell "Mary's old typewriter." I had loaned them my old Remington portable when I was over there staying with them, but I was glad to give to the cause. I had never seen Cape Cod before. The fliver puttered away across the bare, bold headlands, facing the shining sea. A deer bounded across the dirt road in front of us and I found myself rejoicing in my new company.

At dinnertime, I was introduced to the ritual. Conrad was walking back and forth in front of the old kitchen range with a cat on his shoulder named, if my memory serves, Miss Mouse. He talked at length about "consciousness," a theme that was none too familiar to me, even if I had gone to Harvard. We drank out of pewter goblets engraved with grape leaves, an obvious connection to the ancient Greeks. It was not too far-fetched an allusion. I later likened this ritual to seabirds rising from their rocky nests in response to the dying sun. But this ceremony continued sometimes for hours before we sat down to eat. These were libations to the gods of creation and, above all, "consciousness." This man, I thought to myself, with his red hair and bull neck, must have an incredibly strong constitution.

Conrad was a man of medium height and heavily built. My sister once said he looked like a "dissipated deacon," with his red complexion and scholarly air. When he spoke or read with pursed lips and careful articulation, he carried a weight of literary allusion with him. His speech was not of Savannah, Georgia, where he was born. It had overtones of old New England, clipped, probing, as exact as he could make it. He told me that when he was young he was extremely shy: "I could hardly bring myself to talk to the butcher."

Mary Aiken was quick. Besides being an artist, she had been a dancer. At times, she was too quick in her judgments of other people, but she could always cheerfully recover. She painted the Cape landscapes of cranberry bogs and old graveyards, as well as bold, open portraits of friends and local characters. She was innately plucky and unfailingly supportive of her husband, whose contradictory moods could not have been easy to live with.

The evening ritual, not to be confused with your average "cocktail hour" in a city apartment, was always to be taken seriously. Conrad was not pleased with guests who refused the libations. Luckily, I was young, strong, and curious. Basic rituals always require depth and continuity. One night, after some steady drinking of the Holy Grail, a drink made of orange juice and a cheap gin called Dixie Bell, the Aikens served a lengthy meal to four guests in addition to the three of us. One exhausted young man slipped quietly under the table. The rest of us were in various stages of silence or incoherent speech. I faced Conrad at the other end of the table. He appeared to be solidly in control of himself. "Well, Conrad," I said, "you and I seem to be the only survivors." The next day I asked him what he proposed to accomplish. Was he in pursuit of some continuous dream at the end of the night, a revelation of the unconscious? He seemed to agree, but I knew my equation lacked authority. Many are deeply afraid of the very idea of searching their own unconscious, but dreams, I began to realize, were never absent, by night or day. It must have been a depth of connection that he was after. Mary once told me that I should get rid of my inhibitions. I tried, but I was only a beginner.

Mary had a small class of art students while I was there, and Conrad had me writing sonnets, a practice in discipline, but the education I was getting from them was far more comprehensive than I realized. Poetry was not to be separated from the art and intensity of life itself. Conrad once told me that poetry, meaning, I think, lyrical poetry, was akin to nonsense verse. He was fond of the comics in the newspaper, as well as the jazz of Duke Ellington and "Satchmo," Louis Armstrong. Lyrical music and poetry must be liberal and free. It must come from the unconscious, though I suspect bad or disturbing dreams were often in his way.

One day we set off in Libido to New Bedford. His uncle

Alfred Potter had died out in California, and his ashes had been shipped east in a box to be buried in the local cemetery. Aiken got out of the car in front of the town hall and proceeded into the Registrar's office. When he emerged, he said the plot for Uncle Alfred, once the librarian of Harvard College, was not ready. He was told to return later on. He came out bearing the precious relic and reported that the box had come open and spilled its contents out over the selectman's desk. He was dazzled by its iridescence, "like a handful of jewels." I was deputized to hold the box on my lap as we drove home, and I was decidedly uneasy about it. Never did death ride so lightly. On our return, Uncle Alfred's ashes were placed on the upper shelf of the coat closet, there to await final internment.

They had a flock of chickens, black-and-white speckled Hamburgs, which Conrad referred to as the "star-spangled hamburgers." I was given the chore of collecting their eggs. Since I had had a flock of white leghorns in New Hampshire, as well as my own pigeons, I had learned how to execute and "dress" them for the kitchen. My other appointed task was to cut brush on their property, which sometimes helped me to recover from the night before.

One rainy evening, a man whose name I no longer remember came in to talk to the Aikens but soon walked out. He said that he would never go there again, even with a ten-foot pole. I never knew why, but I guess he had met with one of Conrad's abrupt and angry moods, reflected in his behavior when he was faced by people who barged in unexpectedly. The inner man, who could not face the butcher, drew back from interlopers. With his close friends and admirers he was full of wit and imagination. He was a man of manners and civility, and his range of experience was such that the beginners like me were drawn to him. I had to go, even before I understood him, and it was likely that I never would. That he could be pugnacious and defensive at unexpected times was not hard to see, but there was a great deal more to him that I failed to understand. I felt that he was constantly measuring his own interior, a passion below the surface. What I did see was that he was no tame and acceptable poet. He battled to hold on to his role in life and his achievements. That kind of commitment was new to me, but I also knew that his own kind of wildness also carried with it a devotion to what his inner nature had sensed as fiery and unfathomable. It meant exploration of a kind that could only be experienced on passionate terms. It was the kind of passion that could easily drive most people off the track, but with the support of his unfailingly courageous and loyal wife, he had begun to settle down (he had been married twice before). I read a novel of his called Blue Voyage, which revealed a level of domestic rancor and ferocity I never wanted to meet.

I think it was later on that I heard the story of how an early experience had shaped his life. His father had been a doctor in Savannah, where the family lived in a handsome house. Dr. Aiken had suspected his wife of exchanging love letters with a man they knew. One day when Conrad and his sister were sitting on the staircase leading to the ground floor, they saw their father shoot his wife and then kill himself. The 11-year-old Conrad, showing great strength of mind and self-control, walked to the police station and informed them.

What happened to him at such an age might have been enough to destroy the stability of a man with half his stamina. The image of his dead mother must have always been with him. In a play he wrote called Mr. Arcularis, which was performed in Provincetown, on the Cape, the protagonist's mother came out of an underworld that holds both the living and the dead. The name Arcularis was taken from the Egyptian book of the dead.

My idea, when inviting myself to stay with the Aikens, was not to learn how to write, but to be encouraged to write as a way of life. I knew very little about either of them to begin with, but they attracted me by their passionate commitment to art. I understood that Aiken was a well-known, established poet, but I had read very little of his poetry. Much of it, when I was in my early twenties, seemed too long and formidable to tackle. (Many years later, he gave my wife and me a copy of his *Collected Poems*. The inscription he wrote, with his saving grace of humor, was "This monstrosity.")

I went to Forty-One Doors because I wanted to see what it was like to live for a while with two creative people who regarded art and literature as an adventure. My upbringing was far from adventurous. I had always been protected from as many risks as possible. The Aikens were both highly civilized people, but it was their quality of daring that attracted me. They had left not one but a number of worlds behind them to find a home together, not free of trouble, but close to an essential space—the sea—where thoughts and imagination were free to travel far beyond the immediate. Still a romantic and idealist, I envied their recklessness.

The following sonnet, "Sonnet I" (from his *And in the Human Heart*), is one of a group of sonnets Conrad wrote for his wife Mary:

Bend as the bow bends, and let fly the shaft,
the strong cord loose its word as light as flame;
speak without cunning, love, as without craft,
careless of answer, as of shame or blame:
this to be known, that love is love, despite
knowledge or ignorance, truth, untruth, despair;
careless of all things, if that love be bright,
careless of hate and fate, careless of care.
Spring the word as it must, the leaf or flower
broken or bruised, yet let it, broken, speak
of time transcending this too transient hour,
and space that finds the beating heart too weak:
thus, and thus only, will our tempest come
by continents of snow to find a home.

They had planned to be buried in Bonaventure Cemetery in Savannah. Their grave lies by a marble table, where they hoped their friends would come to drink to their health and memory. After Conrad died in 1973, Mary had these words carved on the stone: "Cosmic Voyager. Destination Unknown." I who had watched their travels between the known and the unknown was lost in admiration for her beautiful audacity.

Mind
the Gap

AS I WAS GETTING READY TO LEAVE FORTY-ONE DOORS, Conrad said that he felt sorry for any friend of theirs who had to meet the world. I did not really understand what he meant by it, though I recognized that the world, as always, was a dangerous place, full of threats and treachery, no haven for the shy and retiring. In his case, it might have meant a dispossession of the spirit in a world that made a mockery of dreams. All I knew was that the future was still open to me and that what had sustained me so far might last indefinitely.

I soon discovered that the official world, as represented by hundreds of GIs in an army camp, was far from threatening. The routine was tedious and uncompromising, and what my new friends said about Fort Jackson, S.C., would make a maiden blush. Their language enriched my vocabulary. Infantry camp was a dry and dusty place without a blade of grass, except in front of the officers' quarters.

There are always endless reasons to gripe about life in an army camp, but you make the most of adversity and even find some pride in it that is often lacking in the world outside. The spontaneity with which I found friends was new to me. I landed there with young Americans from small towns all over the country, from rural areas and big cities. In the barracks there were men from the lower east side of Manhattan, together with others from the hills of Tennessee. After some months with them I was transferred to army intelligence because of my brief experience as a Washington correspondent. I became an editor of *Yank*, the army weekly in New York, which was no hardship, and was later sent from there to Panama to be its Central American editor. This was an area in which the GIs stationed in coast artillery posts found life so flat and uneventful that some of them longed for the Japanese to fly in and attack.

But my heart went back to the men of the Eighth Infantry Division. They had been transferred to the western front, whereupon the Eighth Infantry was so emptied of men that it had to be reorganized several times over. Perhaps the darkest part of the war comes to most men from the loss of their friends in combat. In modern warfare, where whole societies are uprooted and disengaged from their own lands, the numbers of the dead are counted every day, but it is the single death that counts the most.

The sheer weight and extent of World War II served to accelerate a process of universal dislocation. Not long ago, I was standing in line at the town hall and I heard a woman who had emigrated from Estonia saying, "The Russians ran over us, the war has never ended." The war created chasms between people and their lands that were not soon bridged. The reality of a home well lodged in nature and history was becoming less tangible.

After the underground terror of the totalitarian states, after the death camps—Dachau, Belsen, Buchenwald, Auschwitz—came the mushroom cloud, the blinding flash of the atom bomb, visited on the unsuspecting people of Hiroshima and Nagasaki. Hatched in the beautiful mountains of New Mexico. The atomic physicist Robert Oppenheimer, when watching the first successful test of this ultimate weapon, quoted a line from the Upanishads: "I am become Vishnu, destroyer of worlds." Most of us felt little alternative but to believe that the use of the atom bomb was justified if it shortened the war. Yet how were we to accept this new role for the human race, faced with the prospect of general annihilation disguised as security?

At some time during the war, which like all wars imposed its own rules, I had the feeling that we were all hanging on an edge of time and that all seasons were subject to arbitrary change. At each station of the London underground (or "tube"), just as the train slows down before stopping, the conductor calls, "Mind the gap." This is a warning to the passengers to be careful when stepping over the opening between the cars and the platform. It seemed to me that a gap in time between us and our expectations had widened into a pit. I saw the past as I had known it rushing away, like the last car disappearing down the curving darkness of the tunnel.

"The Lord giveth and the Lord taketh away. Blessed be the name of the Lord." So it said in the Bible. But when Man takes on the mantle of the Lord, what peace of mind can we expect? I saw myself standing in an empty station waiting for deliverance, like countless people all over Europe.

Going | Home

AFTER I WAS DISCHARGED FROM THE ARMY, MY SENSE OF relief was profound. My wife Kristi and I walked over to Times Square to join the crowd on the night of the armistice. Broadway and the theater district shone with reflected light from the billboards high overhead. We watched the latest news moving by on the Times building. It was a quiet crowd, fairly late at night, after an earlier celebration of victory. I sensed another darkness at our backs borne out of the recent memory of all the friends we had lost and left behind.

"Goodbye to all that," wrote Robert Graves after the first conflagration, only twenty-five years before. On the night of that armistice, Enrico Caruso appeared on the balcony of the Plaza Hotel to sing his heart out. This time I heard no singing. Perhaps whole generations of song and music had disappeared. We were nervous about leaving our baby alone in her crib, so we hurried back to our small apartment, through dark streets, dark history.

The end of the war brought relief, yes, but as I stepped off the curb on a familiar street of storefronts, which looked the same as they always had, I realized that everything had changed. During the war I had felt that it might be possible for modern violence to tip the planet over the edge like some vast table, spilling out its inhabitants to find their way back as best they could. In Europe, millions had been displaced from their native lands, turned almost into planetary wanderers.

We were counting on our country, now a world power, to put things back together; to return, as the establishment had put it in the past, to "normalcy." We had the weight to do it since, according to Robinson Jeffers, America was "thickening to empire."

"Well," I thought to myself, feeling like a child tossed off the merry-go-round, "what should I do with myself now?"

I had been given marching orders for five long years, and when I asked that great world I had been warned against what I should do next, I found it had nothing new to advise, except "Wait." This was backed up by instruments of finality that could not take no for an answer. It gave much courage to Congress to equate finality with security. I was in safe hands, though I knew we had left a terrible waste of men and resources behind us. I thought the war was just and had to be won, but I was also convinced that the world might be sending me on the wrong track.

I had thought for some time about writing a book, to be entitled Looking for My Country, but I soon learned that I had overestimated my capacity to undertake such a task. Anxiety seized me and held on for a long time. Nothing of my original innocence remained. I visited some beautiful parts of the country, notably in the Southwest, where my sister lived with her husband, a native Texan. Traces of the old frontier were still there. I could see out, but never far enough. I drove through a real desert but never set foot in it. I seemed to be wandering in the deserts of my mind. My proposed book should have been called *Looking for Myself*. Finally, I ended up on the freeway heading for Los Angeles at rush hour. A car crossed my bow, crushing the mud-guard, and went on unheeding of my cry of rage. There seemed to be an ambulance waiting every half-mile or so to pick up victims. I turned away, with my back to the Pacific.

Another book on discovering, or rediscovering, America made no sense anymore. I had been like a kid who loved small towns and the wailing of lonely trains off in the hills or over endless, only partly inhabited, spaces. When I was a boy, standing in an open field under the summer sun, I could see all of North America mapped in the passing clouds. Now, it was as if I had been off to the races and lost my shirt.

The country was far too big for me to take it in. Besides, everywhere I traveled I was faced with people who had pulled up stakes and moved on. I found Carl Sandburg's people, but I could seldom catch up with them. We were all on the run, gambling our future to more "progress" and "improvement." I had never wanted to be dispossessed of my origins, but they were being deserted at the speed of light.

After another period of painful indecision, I thought of that "worthless woodlot" I had bought while staying with the Aikens on Cape Cod. There, perhaps, in that quiet and neglected part of the earth, with its low trees and deserted ground, I might find the right direction. I did not know the first thing about that sandy land and its plunging winds from everywhere, but it offered some freedom for the spirit. My education, which was almost completely lacking in sci-ence, held me back. The countryside was being abandoned by its original settlers. The small towns and the family farms were threatened, and the new highway was replacing a wealth of narrow dirt roads. We were happy in our ignorance all the same. We could look out on a vast world sea that promised open-ended answers to our questions. It was time to reach for everything my upbringing and schooling had left out. Life springs from the still unknown. "Ah, but a man's reach should exceed his grasp," wrote Robert Browning, "or what's a heaven for?" I had no conviction as to my chances in heaven, but reach I must, or be abandoned to the whims of a world that could only deliver final answers.

A Sea Change

WE DROVE TO CAPE COD TOWARD THE END OF WINTER, moving into Forty-One Doors while the Aikens were away, so as to watch the construction of our new house on Dry Hill. It was only a mile away as the crow flies. The hill, 120 feet above sea level, stood out like a high sand dune whose slopes were covered by what was called "scrub oak" and pitch pine, as well as thickets of bullbrier and scattered shrubs such as huckleberry and high and low blueberry.

It was a typical postglacial landscape, full of low hills, gullies, and ravines descending to areas of freshwater marshes and bogs. To some outsiders it must have looked almost poverty stricken. There were, and still are, many acres behind our house site that look like an abandoned battlefield, dark ground full of oaks in various stages of decay. I could push many of them over by hand. This poor part of the land was the center of what the locals called a "worthless wood-lot." They had given up on it, having been at work cutting the trees down for several centuries, since the first settlers arrived.

I had paid twenty-five dollars an acre for the land. I was told that it amounted to ten acres, "more or less," but when my first tax bill came, amounting to almost four dollars, I found that the town was charging me for eighteen acres "more or less," so I had picked up eight for free. The prospect of living in paradise did not require much money. We were not poor, since we had enough to build a house, but we were not so rich as to be able to hide ourselves from where we stood. The low-growing trees of the Cape were the result of repeated cutting. The oaks were allowed to grow again "from the stump," often branching out from several trunks. So the Cape had been reduced to bare land, looking out on an open sea. Now that its early conquest was over, at least for the time being, we rejoiced in what was left, as we looked out on a New World that could justify its name.

After our first night in the new house we woke up to the wonderful bugling of a flock of Canada geese flying by the open window. Knowing nothing about their reputation for spoiling lawns and golf courses, we welcomed them as mirrors of the wild, travelers for a still-untamed continent. Later, as spring progressed, that great American bird the ruffed grouse drummed in the season from a stone wall we were building outside the house, while several deer browsed at the edge of the clearing.

One day, two venturesome women drove up the old dirt woodlot road that led to the house. Bold as brass, without wasting any time knocking at the front door, they climbed out of a battered Chevy and took a look around. When I came out, they explained that they wanted to see why in the world anyone would want to build a house in such a bare and wasted-looking place. "We have concluded," one of them said as they were climbing back into their car, "that it must be the view." And that was the last we saw of them.

There was a hint of suspicion in that brief visit. As I thought about it later on, they were not out to welcome us into the neighborhood. It was their view they were concerned about, not ours. Their view had been opened by their ancestors. Cape Cod had been stripped of its trees, and what they looked out at, or hid from, was the stormy sea.

The small towns on the Cape did not necessarily welcome each other. They had a history of independence and found it difficult to plan together. Rivalry was more common than unity. That gave the towns a certain distinction, an identity of their own, which they could not easily part with. After the war, as newcomers were just starting to pour in, it was said in one town meeting that the moderator refused to recognize a resident, stopping him short as he rose to speak with "Sit down, stranger."

I remember visiting a small town in rural Mississippi where a man in a bar, after being introduced to me, said, "Tell me. Why does everything have to come from New York?"

It might have seemed to many year-round residents of the Cape that New York was coming too close for comfort. When the summer ended they said goodbye to all the New Yorkers with at least a pretense of relief, but the old Cape was never entirely abandoned by the city. It had been a haven for artists and writers for two centuries. They stayed there, or they returned, to live near the fishermen of the sea and shore, because the Cape was "way out," still lying off like an arm in the sea beyond the reach of improvement and progress.

What I had looked for was not to "get away" so much as to move in, to a land that was not yet separated from the sea that surrounded it. In a sense I was only going back to the point at which I was separated from it. I had a whole lifetime ahead to be exposed to the endless detail and majesty of what I had neglected.

In late winter the fog stood in between the wet, dark trunks of the worthless trees like smoke. They too were residents, though I did not know them. They were not timeless in themselves, but in their tough and native way they sensed where they ought to be, making their stand within the limits of a land made up of sand and tidal waters that remained essentially what it had always been. Its history was in the tides.

No matter how many demands we made on the land, it had been born of the sea and would eventually be buried by it. The Atlantic Ocean, the great common denominator, was never absent, no matter how much we tried to hide ourselves from it. You could smell salt air on the wind. The outer sandy reaches were endlessly exposed to the power of a storm, or the brilliance of the rising and setting sun. The ocean never tolerated temporary possession such as ours. Its standards, as the original wilderness, were severe, while its capacity to contain was immeasurable.

The great motion of the planet in the rise and fall of the tides, the seasonal violence of late winter and spring, simply carried out the terms this wilderness demanded, a coexistence impossible for us to equal. We might label everything in sight, but we had to learn about ourselves and the land on its own terms.

When a last fiery tumult graced the horizon at sundown, we retreated into darkness, with the sound of the sea breathing in the distance. I walked one day with a Frenchman by birth on top of the high cliffs that stand over Nauset Beach. Looking out over the uninterrupted expanse of saltwater before us, he said, "Grand et large" as he held out his arms in a gesture of praise.

The sea will not accept death even at the hands of those who impose it on her. Transformation is all.

The Nearness of the Universe

AFTER MANY DAYS OF GRAY SEA WEATHER, COLD FOG hanging between the trees, plus sleet and rain, the north wind blew in and snow fell everywhere over this land in the sea. After the storm was over, I walked out into the night. The dark ground was lost under a pure white coating of snow, which was crossed by long shadows from the trees as straight and distinct as the truth. The sky was crystal clear. I looked up with a strange, wild feeling of exhilaration at all the stars. They were very large and brilliant in their tall heaven, almost close enough to touch.

This was infinity enough. What did I need to know about the conquest of space? I was already there. I did not need to travel much farther than where I stood, sheltered by a stream of starry light.

I had read about the expanding universe. Later on, I heard that it was actually shrinking. Perhaps the end of the universe, like some giant canyon rim looking out on nowhere, was no end at all, or one that was impossible to cross. I had been flung out and returned to Earth, part of the process of perpetual renewal. I shared my existence with all other forms of life and states of being. Outside of them I was nothing. It was the nearness of the universe that held me fast.

Way out there was the constellation of Pisces, lying directly south of Andromeda on an apparent path between Aries and Aquarius. Pisces, so I found out, has no exceptionally bright stars but is united by a wavy band, which might have been seen in ancient times as the wavy tail of a fish.

It was now mid-April and I could hear the mewing and calling of herring gulls, coming in both from the east and west of our hill. I walked down to Stony Brook Road and headed toward the Herring Run, a well known land mark in town; and it was there that I really began to embark on my new learning.

On the
Edge

I AM, AFTER A LIFETIME, STARTING—IN THE SAME PLACE where I began—to move out and discover the worlds of life that had begun to reveal themselves. I am in a dingy wood, full of dead and dying trees; they look as if they had endured some catastrophic event. There are many reasons for it. The trees have been cut down and cut again for firewood during the past few centuries. Periodic plagues of gypsy moths have weakened them. They are full of insect borers and fungus diseases. I have been pushing the dead ones down for fifty years. The land is dry and sandy. Salt spray drives in from the sea on any storm. The scanty woodland is only a patch of Cape Cod as a whole, but it seems at times to represent a last holdout of an ephemeral land whose shores are constantly being worn away.

A cold night in late fall, and the moon shines through the foggy air. The backwoods glimmer in its light. If you came into this gaunt woodland by accident you might feel you were irretrievably lost. All the old footpaths and trails can still be traced, but they mean little to a society that builds roads across them, insisting on "improvement." "What is there," the trees seem to say, "to improve?" This is a place, like so many across the earth, that is in the grips of a "recovery" that is too far in the distant future for me to understand. It harbors a loneliness that our crowded world avoids like the plague. But what does not grow out of darkness? It is necessity that puts the frantic, disturbed human race on the same level as the ant, or the pill bug in rotting wood. The night stands against all our artificiality. We are unable to answer back.

In November, a month for migrants and wanderers, I have become aware of the fierce standards that govern life in our undeveloped woodland. Possibly because so many regions have lost their predators, such as owls, bobcats, foxes, and other meat eaters, the opossums have moved into new regions of America. I was not aware that they had begun to populate these shores until I saw a dead one being washed and rolled around in the surf.

One evening, our spaniel, an old dog of eleven years, brought in a limp and bow-shaped body in its jaws. It was a young one, white-furred, with a scaly tail and a pointed, narrow face. The dog then brought in two more on the following days, and once he returned smelling of dead meat, in which dogs delight in rolling. They were all young, but if it was a common family catastrophe, I could not locate it. I found no hollow tree. Perhaps the female died somewhere in the very long stone wall that moves down to the small bog out of the hillside slopes of a glacial hollow. Opossums favor areas where some source of water is nearby.

The opossum is famous for "playing dead." It is an inoffensive animal, slower than most of its predators. When faced with one, unable to run away, it goes into a catatonic state, with various degrees of suspension of bodily activity. Opossums may freeze when faced unexpectedly by a dog—a major enemy—or they may subside into a state of inanimate suspension that may last for several hours. Because the opossum is an animal that is too slow to outrun its predators, unless it is close to a tree or a deep hole it has no main defense except to freeze. Our own dog, who eats dead meat with alacrity, is unable to tell the difference, or respect it. For the poor opossum, "playing dead" is a last resort that does not guarantee success.

Opossums are nocturnal wanderers and their night vision is very keen, as is their hearing, which at least helps them to keep away from danger. Their sense of smell is also well developed. But, and alas, from our perspective, it has a low IQ. The cranial capacity of a raccoon, in one experiment, was found to contain 150 beans, whereas an opossum's skull holds only 21. This might suggest that you do not need high intelligence in order to survive. A friend with a somewhat cynical view of her fellow beings once told me, as I repeated these statistics, "That's perfectly obvious."

If the opossum does not count on brains to survive, it can count on its fecundity. The female, a marsupial, meaning the young are carried in a pouch, can feed up to thirteen young, eight or nine of which might be born in one litter. They will grow to have fifty teeth, as compared to thirty-two in ourselves. They will eat vast numbers of insects of all kinds, as well as earthworms and carrion. So this non-aggressive and relatively slow-moving creature, with two litters a year, manages to pull through. I suspect we need the gentler species as a basis of comparison to all those we admire so much for their quickness and ferocity.

In any case, I feel highly sympathetic toward these small animals of supposedly lesser worth. It is probable that most of them do not last more than two years. Winter is especially hard on them, when the food supply is locked in by snow and frozen earth, especially in their northern ranges. With their short legs, they can be greatly hampered during a season of deep snow. Many die during protracted periods of freezing weather. Sometimes their scaly tails are so frozen that they lose them.

In his book *Of Men and Marshes*, published in 1957, Paul Errington described the harsh and unforgiving conditions experienced by muskrats during winter in the Midwest:

Here is a beaten group trying to weather a cold snap. They huddle, a half dozen of them, in the catch-out and reworked shell of a small lodge. Some openings to the outside are plugged with mud fragments of waterlily root sticks and miscellaneous debris, even with frozen bodies of bullheads. Other openings are partly plugged; others are not plugged at all, and inside the muskrats sit with upper parts frozen and lower parts wet. The inside ice glaze has bullhead bodies in it but the muskrats are no longer eating them. They are no longer doing anything but sitting or rearranging themselves. A wet tail tip sticks out of the opening and freezes to the ice outside. I have stroked the backs of such animals with a hatchet handle, and they just turned to look at me, without otherwise moving.

Next morning, the whole top of the lodge shell is open, empty of muskrats, and powdered by the trace of snow. A mink-killed muskrat lies smeared with blood on the ice, and a drag trail represents another victim. A third muskrat lies on the ice without a wound on it, but with its lungs congested from pneumonia. The trail of a live muskrat can barely be distinguished after tracking around the wreckage of the lodge, the animal headed for the shore, where it worked the rushy and woody fringes before crawling under a boat. (Paul Errington, *Of Men and Marshes* [New York: MacMillan Company, 1957], p. 50.)

I do not see how anyone reading these blunt phrases about the plight of these desperate animals in midcentral, northern winter marshes can help having a sense of profound vulnerability. We too are victims, though we spend all our wealth and power trying to hide it from ourselves. The human world persists in the illusion that the earth can be shaped in its favor. The idea that nature is cruel invades our minds to the extent that we dismiss it; nature is without validity to a world that removes it from sight.

But ultimate truths live under all we hide or repress. The animal lodges we occupy, well heated and protected, are never entirely free of ice and the greater powers of the north. In setting ourselves apart from the rest of living creatures, we instead fall victims to our own ice-bound conceit. It is only in sharing that we know anything at all.

Poverty Grass

IT HELPED A GREAT DEAL TO HAVE COME TO A RELA-
tively impoverished and abandoned piece of land. If it could
be called poverty stricken, that allied it with what the native
Cape Codders called "poverty grass," a species of *Hudsonia*, or
beach heather, that grew in the sand dunes. We had enough
money to build our house and pay the bills, but what the
land could tell me seemed infinitely more valuable.

I came there carrying much twentieth-century baggage
with me that I could not dispense with all at once, but
I began to see what was missing in my education from the
beginning. This was not man's world, or even "nature" in
our sense of the term, that I was beginning to respect and
sort out. All the life I had never stopped for, in every detail,

hidden or on the surface, and that I had dismissed as "only" a leaf or a butterfly, now materialized as if for the first time. There was not time to lose. It was as if I had been taught all I knew up to that point by an elementary school that ignored the elements.

The
Natives

THE WINTER AFTER WE SETTLED INTO OUR HOUSE ON
Dry Hill, there was a period in late winter when the snow
fell for what must have been two days and nights. The local
road, Stony Brook, was impassable. The neighbors, most of
whom we had never met before, started to shovel out the
high drifts to open the road. A snowplow had come in and
broken down completely. I found nuts and bolts strewn
liberally over the surface of the road.

A friend, a young writer I had just met, and I set to work
with our snow shovels. The real natives were on one end
and the newcomers on the other. We had cleared out about
a quarter of a mile when rescue arrived in the form of a
snowplow with more stamina. The shovelers retreated. I do

not remember exchanging a word with my neighbors. Getting acquainted took time and patience in those days.

"Most men," wrote Henry Thoreau, thinking, I imagine, of his taciturn New England neighbors, "live lives of quiet desperation." I knew them as a boy, in both Massachusetts and New Hampshire. They only said what they felt was pertinent to any given occasion. Why waste time on anything but the essentials? Still, I think they were far less desperate than the new generation of country people who struggle with an outside world that is always trying to disengage them from the essentials of what makes life worth living. In that earlier time, the natives had a future when they had lived in a place long enough to accumulate a past. Directions for a long life came as a result of association. The land belonged to those who held its truth inside them.

Cape Cod natives, perhaps because they didn't have to contend with rock-cold winters, seemed to be more easygoing than our neighbors to the north. They were sea and shore fishermen and "truck gardeners," growing and selling potatoes and turnips, strawberries and cranberries.

Brewster was a small town, with about 900 inhabitants. So few cars went by that it was possible on some side roads to play marbles or jackstraws on their surface with impunity. After the end of summer, when all the tourists left, the proprietor of the local country store would sigh with relief. And the sky would turn a brighter shade of blue.

Donald Doane was his name. Next to his store was a very small post office. One day, someone from New Jersey, a menacing state in those innocent times, found the post office closed. So she went next door and consulted Donald, who told her that he did not sell stamps.

"How come," she asked, "you sell postcards, but you don't sell stamps?"

He replied, "Well, I sell toilet paper, but I don't sell toilets."

Minding one's own business was a practice that grew less popular in later years.

Nate Black, whose house was on the dirt road below Dry Hill, made almost daily trips to the shore to dig clams. He also had a small barber shop outside his house, where you could get your hair cut for only fifty cents. He had a flock of chickens that wandered around the yard, and so did we, for many years. Nate was said to have Indian blood in him. So did Jesse Alexander, the wife of Harry, the alewife warden. Harry was the first to tell me what part of the pond shores to visit if I wanted to see the alewives in the act of spawning. He was also my first authority on the subject of the Run. He referred to the young alewives hatched in the ponds as "youngsters"—his youngsters. He was proud of having lived a long and sometimes boisterous life, not devoid of alcohol. He had a strong sense of humor and a passion for his own locality.

"Now," he said, "listen to me. There are too many people coming into town these days who think they know more than we do. Let's get this grand old town back the way it used to be. See what I mean?" Harry, I miss you.

Ring Around
the Moon

ORIGINALLY, I HAD BOUGHT DRY HILL ALMOST BY ACCI-
dent, leaving open the possibility that I might be able to
count on it later. When we finally moved in, I realized that
the space it offered was not of my own choosing. We looked
down from Dry Hill, 120 feet above sea level—high for a
land of low glacial hills and sand dunes—and saw the narrow peninsula of the Cape as nothing more nor less than the
servant of the sea. We could only listen and wait for what it
had to tell us. Every surrounding detail, from a leaf to a
grain of sand, must answer to its laws. The tides along the
rippling shores did not accept man-made time for their
measure. Endless motion was behind them. I began to see
how dependent we were on what we never made our own.
Our world could cover Cape Cod with houses and highways

and conveniences, but they would all be temporary. I listened to the unconquerable, long sound of the surf in the distance.

A winter storm moved in. We could hear its low, hollow booming in the trees. This typical "nor'easter" produced a frothing white mass on the beaches, took away tons of sand from both the inner and outer sides of the Cape, and then, after several days, subsided at nightfall. No man could turn it back. It was by such a measure that the land was first created and would eventually be submerged.

After dark, the moon shone out brightly through the hazy sky, and around it was a great white circle. It may have been that in the high, thin air, where it was extremely cold because of the coming of a new cold front from Canada, the clouds had been frozen into this brilliant alliance with moonlight. I was transfixed by it, dazzled and held in compliance with all I could not reach or entirely understand. That frozen image, hanging like some symbol over the waters of the sea world beyond us, put all ideas of the conquest of nature out of my mind.

Migration

A FEW PEOPLE THOUGHT THERE WAS SOMETHING VERY repetitious and uninteresting about the annual migration of the "herrin." They were "only fish," after all, without much choice in what they did. That we too might always be doing the same thing is not what we like to think about, because that deprives us of the illusion of free will.

Still, for me, the real wonder of the herring lay in the ancient power of their mission, which, like birth itself, escaped any easy definition. In essence, the migration, however simple it might seem to us, involved a coastline that was thousands of miles long. Each local stock moved in during early spring to find "the home stream," where they had been hatched and started to grow.

The transition between saltwater and fresh, aside from

what inland obstacles the herring might encounter, involved a physiological barrier. To stay too long in freshwater ponds or lakes was a danger. Alewives landlocked in the Great Lakes were much smaller than the marine variety. They not only risked being stunted, some were also infected by growths of fungi, though this was cured upon their reentering the sea.

The annual migrations of salmon, sea turtles, and seabirds might be far more dramatic in their extent but, as I looked down Stony Brook Valley toward the sea the alewives came from, I saw that they had a stature born of primal risk. In their less conscious way, they were as adventurous as Ernest Shackleton and his men on the *Endurance*.

One day, I watched while a few alewives taken from the Run—the stream and marsh channel between salt- and freshwater systems that the fish followed during their migratory season—were temporarily placed in a freshwater aquarium, for the purpose, I guess, of observation. I was immediately aware that the fish were still on their migration. Their large, open, lidless eyes stared straight ahead. Their silvery bodies, facets of sea light, were tense with purpose. They were moving on to the measure of a power and energy that could never be replaced by anything so temporary as opinions of them. The "herrin" were not "just fish." They belonged to a higher order of migrants that had been exploring our continental limits for an incalculable period of time.

I think there may be some truth in saying that America is now more and more on the run, but in a state of detachment at the same time. We can uproot ourselves from wherever we set down, but it is like leaving life itself to be able—mechanically, at least—to desert a land which is our home. What future can there be which denies its inheritance of the imperatives and directions of the earth itself?

Worlds Without End

THE TOWN OF BREWSTER HAD A POPULATION OF 900 when we came on the scene. This was to climb to a year-round population of 10,000 by the end of the century. Many New England towns, born of the industrial age, were far more populated at an earlier date. Brewster was a "back-water" village for a long time, hard to reach from the mainland until the Cape Cod Canal, its bridge, an intersection, and a new highway were constructed. "Improvement" began to redesign the narrow land and control its future. Old Indian burying grounds were reburied under the bulldozers, dirt roads were replaced with asphalt for modern traffic, while old trails and footpaths were lost and forgotten.

We were the forerunners of a wave that would eventually bury the evidence of local living, a way of life that was simple, from a modern perspective, but attached. Then, you could still count on native dialect, humor, and habit to tell you where the roots were. The land we found, much of it still bare after centuries of tree cutting and subsistence farming, was as open to human domination and possession as any other, but there was something special about it that was past capturing. It seemed to be waiting whatever time might be needed to express its own nature. I saw this long, narrow peninsula held in the arms of the sea as if it were a ship at anchor, ready to take sail, to spread its wings on the sea wind. The land was always in motion, like the waves that were continually taking the far horizon out of sight.

For a while at least, before we were obliged to pay lip service to growing traffic, noise, and the daily news, we were given the time all nature needs to find itself. Although I never knew at first what I wanted to do, or how to fill the gaps the world had put in my way, I began, though slowly, to move toward a wider realm. Daily living, of course, was full of frustration, suspicion, and envy, but that is the way we always begin to navigate in any new place. The sea winds climbed our hill to bring news of all they touched. I began to look in and under as well as out, drawn in by this "worthless" place and what it had to tell me about the terms of permanence. Neither land nor sea could answer to the terms we applied to them in our world. Every detail, I began to see, could only answer to an order that was timeless. Any ignored detail might be an opening to all others.

The shores of Cape Cod Bay were only half a mile away. I had been to the edge of the sea many times before, but I knew very little about the life it held. I walked down to the beach, not to identify anything but to feel the pull of the waves, pulling me outwards, sending me back again, like a sanderling skittering along the sands, a toy on wheels, then picking up quickly and vanishing, out of sight, out of mind. The marine world was full of followers I had never met.

The sands at low tide were covered with chainlike ripple marks left by the dynamic motion of the waves. They seemed to carry me toward some illusory distance just as they had when I was a boy. I had been sent ahead, in a way that fed my aspirations, but I also sensed an impermanence in myself, a cutting off, that was intolerable. It was as if nothing in my education had brought me into constancy, the immediate, like the sand grains, or the salt-marsh grass. I needed fish to tell me where they came from. I wanted the trees to tell me, not invented medicine, where to look for the secret of longevity. Here, at last, was a place where life was new again, and open to the unknown.

I began to see that nothing really stopped for our benefit. The sound of the surf, always booming or chanting on the long shores, came out of the pulsing waves, landing on the beaches in an untiring response to the revolution of the earth around the sun. You had to hold your breath while listening to the waves landing on the beach. They carried the sound of timelessness.

I was not the son of a fisherman. I had no relatives who risked their lives on the constant presence of fish. The fish I knew the best were those I caught along the shores of Lake Sunapee. Before I knew the difference between one species and another, the lake initiated me into the mysterious realms that protected them. As a boy, abandoned to the city in winter months, I would think of the black, or big mouth, bass that were lying suspended under a ceiling of ice. I used to fish for them with rod and line and a hook baited with earthworms, either from our boat dock or the rowboat. In summer, they would lie offshore waiting for prey, close in color and hue to the green mosses and the dark shadows of the hemlocks standing tall above the banks. They were of a live ancestry thousands of years old. I smelled them as I smelled pine sap and needles. As a food, they had no equal. Their flesh, white with delicate black veins, was best cooked over a campfire, under the pines.

There was a sliver of a beach lying along the shore of the lake where we went swimming. The bottom was composed of pure white sand, littered only with a bit of driftwood from the wooded shore. This was where the little sunfish, or "punkin seeds," came to make their nests, slight hollows in the sand. I never knew quite what they were doing, but they hovered over the bottom fanning their tails in a gentle and ceremonious fashion. They are still as clear in my memory as plates of shiny mica or white quartz crystals, taking on the orange sunset on a mountain evening.

These were as direct as I ever came to real fish, out of living water. There was always an unknown, unmet quality to those I glimpsed from the surface. They were treasures, always in hiding, but out in the open I knew them not.

Then, after our first winter on the Cape, I met fish, as if for the first time. I walked down Stony Brook Road, where the Aikens lived, to visit the herring run. It was in early spring, and I could hear all the gulls filling the air with their hunting, quarrelling calls. So I came into a storm of fishes making its way inland from the bay. The fish ladders, concrete pools built to rest the fish on their migratory journey, were packed with shiny dark bodies. The alewives, or freshwater herring, I was to learn, moved inland out of the sea when the fresh waters of the down-flowing brook were warm enough to start them coming in to spawn in a chain of ponds that were the headwaters of the brook.

Those were the rudimentary facts, but as time went on, I began to see them, in their crowded, elementary forms, big eyes always staring ahead, as forerunners of all the powers of the season. I stood on the banks observing that unswerving passion of theirs obeying some imperative darkness I could not try to name. I was told that what I saw represented blind obedience to the reproductive drive, simple enough, like sex. But the questions that came up in my mind were not answered so easily. We tend to see something automatic in them, as if there were no escape, no alternatives in their lives. They do what they have to do, and that is to be forced into unanimity by some iron imperative they cannot escape.

As I looked down at them, all the same, I saw nothing helpless. Those slippery, silvery bodies, held in by the length and width of an inland brook, expressed a desire of the deepest kind. It was the same thing I had glimpsed as a boy: an emergence of life out of the unseen. The greater motions of the sea were in those packed, shiny bodies, and it—the glimpse—led me in and not away.

Above all, I began to see motion as I had never consciously seen it before, a star-struck and wild accommodation to what had always been at a distance from me. I walked downstream where the brook began to wind through the marshes above the shore, and there I met the vanguard of an army. The gulls kept them spread out below the headwaters, but as they came in toward falling water, the multitudes ahead of them waiting to move up and out into the headwaters, they were ranked in almost military discipline. It was like seeing some long-gone Army of the Republic reappearing out of nowhere. I was turned into a conscript once again.

As I followed them in and out in later years, I also saw that they were highly sensitive to their surroundings, and to each other. Their movements at all times of the day reflected where they swam. They swung away from light reflected on the surface. They found safety from the gulls in darker pools, and though they were sometimes caught between tides as they came in, dying in too-shallow waters, they were always awake, pliant, and ready for change. They were obedient to thousands of years of passage from the ocean to the streams and rivers that ran through coastal regions, each one different in its chemical composition from all the others. Alewives accomplished a variousness and an order I never knew existed, though like a fish, I might have sensed it. Fish are not simply captives of their environment. They express its constant changes in themselves.

The ancients who put Pisces in their zodiac found no barriers between fish and the stars. They included the dim image of a fish tail in the heavens, and it was as great a reach of Earth senses as can be accomplished by a modern telescope. They understood that the waterways in the heavens reflected those on Earth. We have lost and betrayed so many fish and fishing people that we begin to see them as being as isolated as our own lives have become. Yet it is the great unknown reaches of the planet that can call fish or men into being. The tides still move in the dark of the moon, and the response of fish to all the waters follows the breath of life.

The earth is held together by its magic retainers, whether they find their homes in rocky pools speckled with light or in the darkness of the seas. I had seldom thought of the inseparable bond between a bird, a fish, or a plant and the earth in terms of the weather, but it is in the wings of a bird, the bark of a tree, the form and body of a fish. And that alliance, I began to see, was almost miraculous and certainly escaped our definitions of it. The idea, in nature, is to live again.

Berry's Hole

I KNEW VERY LITTLE ABOUT THREATENED AND ENDAN-
gered species before we moved to the Cape. I associated
extinction with dinosaurs and the dodo, whatever that was.
Later on, I became very much aware of what had happened
to the passenger pigeon, which had once darkened the skies
of America, a beautiful, much-admired bird, so numerous
that killing it was irresistible. The buffalo, the life and main-
stay of the Plains Indians, just escaped extinction at the
hands of a careless, gambling nation that allowed visiting
noblemen to shoot them for sport from railway trains.

Then there was Buffalo Bill Cody, of the mustachio and
Wild West show, who boasted of having killed 5000 buffalo
on the plains. Buffalo Bill Cody's show included, among a
number of other attractions, an Indian with the once-proud

name of Sitting Bull, who had vanquished General George Armstrong Custer at the battle of the Little Big Horn. Some, including Ernest Thompson Seton, lover and student of the wild animals and America, found the general distasteful. Yet wild animals were a great show in those days, almost like Mother Nature herself. Her progeny also included vast numbers of egrets, terns, and other shorebirds, killed off for the millinery trade.

Cape Cod suffered careless losses too. The black-crowned night heron that fished along rivers and creeks past twilight was once associated with other creatures of the night, such as tiches and lost souls. By day, these birds were called "shitepokes" or "quawks" for their cry. Someone from New York City found a local rookery much too noisy and dirty and perhaps even hazardous, so a game warden by the name of Red Madden was called in, who came in and shot most of them off. I counted 150 bodies lying in the pine woods where their rookery had been. They never returned, though a comparative few nested in some other area back of the shore.

That great American bird the ruffed grouse once graced our presence with its spring drumming on the stone wall outside. In later years, many other ground-nesting birds, oven birds, wood thrushes, and whippoorwills—all great night criers—began to die out as well. A changing habitat, as was originally suggested, was not the cause. They were the victims of the domestic cat, a household pet introduced to the narrow land by the rapid growth of suburbia.

Clint Eldridge, an old Cape Cod neighbor I always liked, used to shoot otters, once common in the Cape's marsh-lands and its waterways. I once saw a pelt he had left in the town dump. It seemed natural to take advantage of re-sources that once had been numerous, even the fish the local fishermen trapped in nets along the shores. The less we lived with abundance, the less we knew it. An emptiness began to spread like a tide out of control and the worst thing about it was our indifference. "This is a beautiful country," said an old Maine friend. "Why do we have to trash it?"

A deep glacial hollow lies below our house, known locally as Berry's Hole. It was named after a native long since dead who once tended a small cranberry bog down there. It is surrounded on all sides by steep hillsides, which give it the appearance of an amphitheater meant for tragic or comic plays and timeless ceremony.

Few people go to Berry's Hole now. The bog is no longer worked, the old wood roads seldom used or else buried in developments. Any open land is referred to by the developers as "raw"; its value lies in its replacement. But the hollow retains a supreme capacity to receive and to protect.

On a bright afternoon in March, I took a walk down the wood road that runs along the upper side of the hollow. Passing where a fox had crossed the road, I smelled its familiar scent and then found, further on, its narrow trail through the tan oak leaves that covered all the ground. It had been a mild winter, with little snow but many rains, and shallow water, deeper on the fringes, covered the bog. The light had reached a new level of intensity, and scattered across the water I heard the rapid clacking and clattering voices of the wood frogs. This beautiful little tan animal, with its black mask, moves out of a winter silence of leaves, near the roots of trees, to start its spring courtship and egg laying, attaching its numerous eggs to submerged vegetation in the bog. So, the great choral ushering in of spring was under way once more. The great stage had opened to what we are meant to hear, the voices of resurrection.

Others join in. Within a few days of the vernal equinox a low, sonorous grunt comes from a bullfrog, holding center stage out on a small island of reeds. Off to one corner of the bog, in a group of swamp maples, tree frogs begin chirping like so many birds. Then, the wild, primal chorus of the *Hyla crucifer*, spring peepers, or pink-winks fills the air.

Their shrill voices are earsplitting. On cold clear nights, I used to take one of our growing children down to Berry's Hole. We would sit on the ground, close to the edge of the bog, with a flashlight, keeping as still as possible. Then we would hear a shrill piping call right next to us from a tiny creature perched on a nearby twig, branch, or blade of tall grass. Out of these choral frogs would come acclamation as wild as the wind. It was as if they meant to pierce the darkness, lifting toward the whiplashing of light between the stars.

One year, long ago, I persuaded two visitors from the Cape Cod Cranberry Company not to spray in Berry's Hole. At that time, DDT was being used on wetlands, including salt marshes and ditches as well as freshwater bogs and ponds, to control mosquitoes. The practice was later abandoned as more and more dead minnows floated to the surface and the marsh fiddler crabs began to disappear.

The two friendly exterminators seemed to agree that the bog would be best protected by its closest inhabitants, the frogs and salamanders. So Berry's Hole, like our worthless woodlot, was left alone. (I might have added, resurrection does not cost that much to maintain.)

For all that, news began to drift in of frogs and toads from various parts of the world dying at an alarming rate. Distortions and malformations were found in frogs all the way from Lake Champlain to wetlands in the Midwest and beyond. (There is a tragic irony in the reported disclosure that infants of farming families have also suffered malformations at birth.) Frogs have sensitive skins, and their eggs are vulnerable to pollutants. It has also been suggested that their decline is the result of global warming and the lethal effect of ultraviolet rays. It may be that industrial and technological advances have also played a major role in the death of certain species. The frogs may be dying out as a consequence of the damage our so-called progress has done to the very tissues of the earth itself. The gap widens between means and ends, between our own bodies and minds and the abstractions we substitute for reality.

All signs point to man as the most visible cause of the death of the frogs. As the list of possible reasons grows to a dismaying length, anyone who still cares is left with the desperate feeling that we may be creating a void between us and the intricate, richly endowed habitats that have endured. The fragile, worldwide interrelationships of aquatic life, which have lasted in both strength and fragility, like spiderwebs in the grass, are being irreparably broken. It seems as if we are mindless resources consuming the living artifacts of creation itself. The evidence is all around us of vast areas of wetland drained of life-giving water, resulting in habitat loss on an unprecedented scale. When marshes and wetlands are robbed of life, it ought to be clear that our own health and future are in jeopardy. A once-timeless, sacred allegiance to the life of which we are a part seems brutally destroyed. Without such moorings of creation, we are all in danger of being lost. Numberless distinct and interdependent ways, all gifts of the land itself, are being stolen by some alien race.

The hours of darkness shorten, and a widening light moves in at an accelerating pace. When the sun rolls in over the horizon it shines over the universal society of life without discrimination. As the wind begins to die down, other voices rise. I hear a gull down in the direction of the herring run. There is a high, excited tone to its call, which I have learned to recognize. It either means there are a few fish in the brook, or that they may be coming. Other gulls gather along the shore in anticipation. A pair of herring gulls fly over my head, engaged in a monosyllabic conversation full of low, almost muttered "wows" and "uh-huhs." It is not hard to believe they might be calling to me as they pass.

A wintering mockingbird flies up into a tree ahead of me and I hear the cheerful notes of a robin with a stronger resonance in its voice. A whole flock of redwings moves back and forth between the thickets on the edge of a small bog by the road. It seems that I am being moved ahead at last to climb the ladders of the coming spring. I have dropped all my assumptions about which, of all species, is the most worthy of our attention.

The Skippers

IT WAS ON THE SEVENTH DAY OF APRIL, MANY YEARS ago. I was walking along the edge of the salt marsh that surrounds Wind Island. On the farther side of the island was Stony Brook and the inlet that brought in the annual run of alewives. Wing Island has a small beach along its outer side facing the bay. The marsh grasses, turned gray by winter weather, were still thick and bending down under their own weight. But it was a warm day and all the marshes were coming alive. Tiny minnows raced ahead of me down the narrow ditches. They made an audible splash as they piled up at the end of a ditch blocked off by grass.

As I walked out to the beach I met two people sitting on the sand. They were David Manville and his wife, of Spencer, Massachusetts, quiet and friendly people, of the kind I knew as a boy, at one with their own land. We talked about the growing pressure and how hard we had to fight to slow it down, foot by foot, yard by yard. That lean and laconic man and his cheerful wife were determined conservationists, of a kind I was trying to enlist as volunteer educators in the natural history museum I had been helping to establish. We needed help and advice from those who knew a land because they were inseparable from it.

I remember his mentioning that he had caught "needlefish" in these tidelands and their inlets but had thrown them back in the water. They were not of any commercial value as food fish. I, for one, had never heard of them. We then spoke of the coming in of coyotes and a loss of foxes. They had sighted deer tracks on the edge of the nearest creek. They were companionable people whom I never saw again, but the needlefish lingered in my mind.

The edge of the sea, as I learned from reading Rachel Carson, is a home for multitudes of living organisms, most of them belonging to species I had never heard of. I had flown across the Atlantic and traveled over it by ship, but what had I seen of its magnitude other than what was washed up on the beach? I had been hidden from this overwhelming capacity to sustain life. It was as if I had been living in a great man-made tunnel designed to cut us off from access to the primal life that should be our everlasting guide. We were all listening to other voices that were disconnected from the sea. From the open end of the tunnel, I heard Jacques Cousteau, announcing the death of the Mediterranean.

It was many years later, early in the month of November, that I first saw the needlefish. My friend North Cairn and I were walking down the beach at East Brewster, having heard that thousands of these little fish had stranded all along the inner curve of the Cape. We began to see their dead bodies scattered across the sand, dematerialized pieces of scale and bone, colorless, meaningless to most beach walkers.

The waves, with a gray-green cast to them, were falling

in at high tide, gently and instrumentally following each other, like revolving mirrors, as they reached the downward sloping beach. Sighting a flash of blue at the water's edge, we leaned down and picked up what we had been looking for, a live needlefish. It had a dark, mineral-blue stripe on its narrow back, like the color of the sky that opens up to the sunlight at the grand parting of dark thunderheads. Its back also had spots of mossy green. The rest of its body was of a startling silver with a golden sheen. The young needlefish are only a few inches long, while the adults might be up to eighteen inches. The term *needle* comes from a protruding mandible, like the elongated bill of a bird. There were so many of them where they lived out in the Atlantic that their numbers could only be estimated.

They were called "skippers," according to Henry Bigelow and William C. Schroeder, editors of the book *Fishes of the Gulf of Maine*, because of their habit of skipping, just short of flying, like the flying fishes, across the surface of the open Atlantic. The young needlefish we saw were stranded in cold waters they could not survive. They were oceanic fish found in the warm currents of the Gulf Stream, out beyond the Cape's bent arm. Inside it, like many other species, including the sea turtles, porpoises, and pilot whales, they are trapped in shallow waters, no deeper than ninety feet, that grow colder in late fall and early winter.

These little jewels, so quick to live, so quick to die, were quite beyond my understanding. It would be easy for us, as members of a supposedly pragmatic and literal-minded society, to put them down as colorful artworks, like the dazzling fish of tropical reefs, but on this gray shore they seemed nothing short of miraculous. What could those tiny eyes see but what the ocean itself made visible out of unfathomable light? The waters of the Atlantic tossed inestimable riches at our feet, and we scarcely noticed them. Under scientific auspices, men might take these jewels for granted, but as an integral part of the vast sea of unknowing, they were miracles.

Inside | the Storm

FOR THE FIRST TIME, THE LAND WE HAD MOVED TO WAS plain enough to read. I began to see ways into an underlying reality I had not been introduced to. Living on the "edge of nowhere" did not cut me off but teased my spirit into the open. Fish, birds, trees, and the weather called for some recognition in me that I had been unwilling or too self-centered to meet. If only one living species like the alewives was able to show me more intricacy and deviation in the land and the waters than I knew how to admit, how wonderfully, at the same time, it was able to free me. My new world, every inch of it, was full of so many unexpected and unanticipated directions that it began to center me in what I now called home. (How could we predict the weather without feeling it in ourselves?)

The fish had begun to reveal themselves to me when they took a course I was unable to predict. It was then that I began to unlock the No Trespassing signs in myself. It seemed to follow that all the life I was starting to recognize was never fixed or finally named; it was answered in the unseen labyrinths of the human spirit. The unknown, the undefeated, was always ahead of us.

During the late fall, going into winter, the wind blew for days on end, stripping the trees of their remaining leaves. Our hill had not been covered with the glorious color of an autumn in New Hampshire. The oak leaves often turned brown before they fell. Strong winds in late October stripped the swamp maples of their leaves, which filled the sky with a yellow rain. Wind from the sea seldom left us. Snowstorms were infrequent because of the warming influence of the sea, but we could expect at least one during the winter.

One morning in mid-December a moderate wind was blowing across the land, but the darkness was setting in and now the wind was banging on the door as if to break it down. Gale-force winds were reported on the radio. A light snow, mixed with sleet, began to fall, and the bare branches of the oaks, reminding me of our own shins, collected a film of ice. Wind-whipped snow was swirling in the air and gathering on the ground. I walked out into the trees and the freezing air cut like a knife. The oaks and some pitch pines had not yet recovered from the wood choppers. They were low-growing and open to any storm. I heard them bending and cracking in that relentless wind, while the sea roared in the distance.

It snowed all day and night and much of the following day. When the storm began to blow out the following afternoon, it was still bitter cold. A labyrinth of blue shadows cast by the trees stretched across the white landscape. The snow had been fashioned into deep drifts outside our house or blown out like shallow waves beyond it, crystalline, impeccable. It seemed like a blessed transformation of the commonplace, the routine difficulties of our lives. For a short while, we were no longer the prisoners of our own distractions. It was exhilarating to exist on this magic new level.

After the storm clouds lifted, the land was almost blinding in the open light. The moon was now hanging out in the freezing air, low on the horizon like an enormous street lamp, lighting the way into the vast impassable sky. How beautiful it was out there, where so little that we knew was able to exist. All things in our land were waiting their moments of silence and their emergence. Just before sundown, the sun's fiery orange deepened as our part of the earth began to retreat and move back into the night. As that great crystal shining disappeared behind the horizon, it left a band of pinkish gray clouds, and a greater silence set in over enameled slopes, as deep as universal, untemporizing law could make it. We go down to sleep in the unfailing light.

The following morning we woke up to the singularity of things outside. I watched a leaf dipping and rising across the snow like a bird. A few hexagonal snowflakes were still falling. A snowflake and a leaf, in a sky-balance with each other, not touching, in a measureless way possible because no one has really proved that each flake is different from any other. The leaf had veins in it like the veins in our hands. They were food and the breath of life to the tree. The uncountable oak leaves covered the ground. Perhaps each one was different from the other as well. The brown oak leaves were like old parchment, where we might be able to read their enigmatic writing. They were to become part of the brown soil, in a state that was neither life nor death but a mysterious merging of both.

A Walk on the Great Beach

BECAUSE I HAD ALWAYS BEEN ATTRACTED TO HEAD-
lands and uninhabited shores, I read Henry Beston's *Outer-
most House* soon after we moved to the Cape. I envied him the
hospitality he found on that lonely but immensely inspiring
shore. You had to go out, as John Muir suggested, in order
to find your way in. So I decided to walk it and get the feel
of it. I started from the beach close to the tip of Provincetown and headed for Nauset Inlet in Eastham, with a light
pack on my back containing enough food to last me a day
or two.

The breakers were pounding in, often sweeping up toward the head of the beach, making me jump out of the
way. I think the city was still in my mind. The surf sounded

like a ton of bricks falling from a building being taken out by a wrecking crew. The unconquered energies of the North Atlantic kept surging in and pounding away at the cliffs, reducing them, so I was told, by an average of four to five feet a year. This was a new way for me to measure a thousand years in a falling wave. My geology was in its infancy, but the Great Beach led toward majestic comparisons in space that no man could alter. We have no rights of possession that are not eventually removed by the sea.

Another time, watching storm waves roaring in from the top of the cliff above the beach, I saw chunks of a continent being reduced to loose sand, falling away to join the beach or be taken offshore by the currents of the tide. Out of the face of the cliff were protruding pipes and hanging telephone wires, some of them lying on the beach. They had come from abandoned cottages originally built to enjoy the view, but this view was never made in so short a time.

I began my walk in the month of June and the Great Beach was almost empty. I walked for miles before I encountered anyone at all. Then I had a brief glimpse of Eden. A young man was standing naked on the beach, with two young women, fully clothed, sitting on the sand behind him. No words passed between us. I greeted them with a raised arm and walked on.

After Cape Cod was designated a national seashore, sleeping at night along the beach was prohibited. I slept in a corner of the dunes, waking up to hear the driver of a beach buggy trying to back out of loose wet sand on a rising tide. When his wheels stopped churning, I fell asleep again, listening to the wind and the beach grasses swishing in my ears, smelling the waters of perpetual motion and irresistible change.

The next day I watched a piping plover, which must have had a nest somewhere in the dunes. It was trying to distract my attention by feigning injury, dragging a broken wing as it edged down toward the surf. No real space was lost between us. I might follow seabirds around the globe, held in measureless containment.

Walking off the Great Beach on that hot June day, I knew I could never answer any of the questions about nature that kept coming into my mind without being aware of a planetary space in terms I could never conceive of. Walking on that lonely beach was to listen to an impenetrable silence behind every wave and gust of wind. The grains of sand that held my body overnight were part of it, just as they belonged to a wearing down of rock and the origin of fire.

We, the survivors of the unseen past, had vital company in the dark. The lone piping plover I had watched as it tried to draw me away from its nest was a keeper of one of Earth's secrets, that of birth itself, a coming into being. Those who share a contempt for animals could never survive without them.

Soon after my walk I learned that the piping plover had been added to the list of threatened and endangered species because of a disturbance of its habitat. For most people, it could have disappeared and they would be none the wiser. Least terns, a small variety with yellow bill and tinkling voice, had several nesting colonies out on the exposed beach, and they too were on the list.

After some protest from the Beach Buggy Association, protective measures were taken, and eventually both the plovers and the least terns began to rebound. The same protection was given to larger species of terns that nested on offshore islands. They were in danger of being forced out of their habitats by herring and great black-backed gulls, whose numbers had grown by leaps and bounds because of the waste food from all our cities, which increased their chances of survival. As winter residents, the gulls were on hand long before the terns came back on their spring migration. Gulls often took over the terns' nesting places and harassed them during the season.

Great Gull Island, located at the entrance to Long Island Sound, several miles off the Connecticut coast, still holds what is left of a fort, long since abandoned. Some thirty years ago, it was bought by the American Museum of Natural History in New York, which established the Great Gull Island program for the protection of common and roseate terns. Helen Hays, the director, taught me far more about her charges than I could ever have learned on my own.

To be in the middle of a tern colony, night and day, was an adventure in recognition that never left me. I never stayed more than a few days on that island without being drawn in by the intensity of those birds. They too were defending the great secret. They were ritualistically engaged. Their courtship flights were strict and beautiful. They rose up from their nests into the air in response to the light of the sun as it left the sea and rose up again at dawn. They defended their chicks with ardor and untiring attention. The adults were unfailing in their fishing flights, bringing back the essential food for their young. The following spring, those juveniles returned to the same small site of grass and sand on stone where they had been hatched. Many thousands of miles were in their minds. They never forgot that site; it was the last place they had heard the voices of their parents.

Birth and death are ceremonials, not confined to the dictates of conscious time. I had not paid much attention to the dawn before I met the terns. They were its true believers. Who was I to refuse them entry into my corner of humanity? They were to carry me further than I had ever been before.

Learning
to Teach

WHEN I WAS GATHERING MATERIAL FOR A BOOK ABOUT the herring run, I met a new acquaintance of ours in the town of Harwich. She told me, with some relish, that she had heard I was writing a book about the sex life of fish. "Is that true?" Well, I supposed, that must be close enough. My favorite aunt, Alice, a sister of my father's, wrote me a letter saying that she could not imagine a more uninteresting subject than fish. She may have respected fishing people and the distant romance of the sea, but what fishermen belonged to was an anonymous realm she had never been encouraged to enter.

About the same period, in the early 1950s, I was asked by a group of people in the town of Dennis to join them in starting a "junior museum." Officers of the new outfit were hastily chosen, and I was secretary for a while, a post that meant little or nothing at the time. Eventually we got around to our purpose, first rejecting the title of "nature center," since it sounded too much like a nudist colony. There was general agreement that it should be a teaching museum. Because we had little money, and few members, we depended entirely on volunteers. What we would teach was wide open to us all, from shore to shore, sea to sea. Natural science was largely left out of the schools, and so we filled a need that was not being met. We began to teach children on the elementary level, taking them out on field trips in the woods, the flats, the ponds and streams where life abounds.

To teach was to be taught. Everyone with enough enthusiasm volunteered to move our museum ahead into new fields, while staying open to what we did not know. Even if many local people did not volunteer or send their kids to our classes in pond life or the salt marshes, the land was still under the influence of people who had lived there for a long time and who were conscious of a common ancestry. Settlement had not yet been succeeded by unsettlement. The people knew identifiable places where you could find clams, oysters, and offshore fishes. They may not have been conservationists in the modern sense, and they were often suspicious of outsiders, but they defended the land through living there. You could even call on their ghosts, if you felt like it.

Those were opening years for me, before we started to be recognized in terms of professional results and reputation. Our board of trustees was composed primarily of educators who had a common enthusiasm, no matter what level of society they came from. Holding or acquiring money seldom fixed them immutably in place, and there was no essential difference between them and the volunteer teachers who were many-sided and enthusiastic with their help.

The natives began to disappear and the outside world

started to come sprawling in, without much sense of where it landed, but that elementary experience stayed with me. It grew slowly, like a tree, but the precedent was made. There was no corner of the land not yet covered by waste that did not bear the signs of life—that was not there for our benefit.

Paine's Creek

THE WIND, WHICH BLEW ALMOST CONSTANTLY AT times during the fall, spring, and winter months, was rattling the windows and filling the house with unexpected sounds. We often woke up just before dawn, a primal event I had neglected in previous years because of an addiction to sleep and schedules. A persimmon bush appeared between the shaking oaks, to be followed by the piercing eye of the sun, casting blue shadows across the snowy ground.

Cape Cod was less covered by people on the run in those days. The natives had not yet fallen victim to outside forces, driven by an empty extravagance that almost moved them and their houses around as if they were on a roulette wheel commanded by distant gamblers. But old communities were losing their common threads of attachment. It was almost as if you could not stay on this narrow peninsula too long or you would be washed away either by the sea or land speculators. Still, there was that which never moved out.

One of the last times I saw Conrad Aiken and his brave wife Mary was in the late afternoon of a day when I had driven them down from Boston; he was old and sick at the time. They brought a thermos containing a gin martini with them, and their purpose was to offer a libation to what never dies.

Since then, I have visited Paine's Creek—where I first saw and felt the alewives moving in—in many seasons of the passing years. The sky and the sea are always changing together, often in multicolored rhythms as the waters of the creek drift and run by to their meetings between saltwater and fresh. The sunsets fill the sky with the fires of their light, orange, yellow, flame-colored bands and leaping forms like great plumes, honoring the approach of darkness and a reverent silence. We tend to be afraid of silence, which really means that we are afraid of ourselves and the loneliness we inspire. Anxiety is constant and makes us run away from where we are, but the night sky in its supreme silence answers all flesh and blood. To go out and listen is to be commanded by an imperishable source that will never answer us on our own terms. "Man invented death," wrote William Butler Yeats. In undying darkness there is no difference between life and death.

Reflections from everywhere ride on the waters. At the mouth of Paine's Creek, where the channel curves and leads into the salt marshes and the gulls wait on the sandbars on their untiring watch, tidewater pushes in from the bay and then retreats, while the waters of Stony Brook run down through the marshes to meet it. Compared with other river mouths and estuaries, for thousands of coastal miles Paine's Creek is only a minor inlet, but as a meeting place between land and sea it also invites many planetary roamers from the sea. It is a link to cosmic histories that far exceed our own.

Toward the end of October I watched the long irregular flights of brant geese as they came in from the nesting grounds in the subarctic to winter on the bay shores of the Cape. A hundred or more of these small, dark geese gathered in a band of marsh grasses that extends behind the narrow beach. I watched them from the dunes, behind marram grass shaking in the wind. The birds grunted to each other, "vocalizing," as the ornithologists put it. They moved slowly among the grasses or swam in the open waters beyond. The brant is a bird of great calm and dignity, with a stocky body and a beautifully carved head. At my human distance and removal, I have always felt honored by their company. "Trrruhk," they call as they fly across the water and over my head. They are not "just birds"; they are distinguished visitors. They come in like other veterans of the continent to take their place in its geography and the unities of land and sea.

Some of the major travelers I learned to watch for were the great white gannets on their southerly migrations from nesting lands in Canada, where they crowd the rocks. They are "plunge divers," folding their great wings and descending like javelins into the surface of the sea to follow schools of fish, leaving white spray at their points of entry. Those birds are spectacular and almost lift me into the air with their great adventure.

Black ducks, eiders, widgeons, old squaw ducks move temporarily into the inlets and marshes for rest, feeding, and shelter. As the rhythm of the year impels their sense of urgency and direction, they move on. For the terns, those buoyant, skillful, and tireless flyers, Cape Cod is not only a place to nest but a way station, a stopover on an endless journey across the seas and around the planet. Who are we, in our idleness, to boast that we surpass them in achievement? The mere presence of such cosmic travelers saves us from confinement.

We are defined as much by changes and transformations

we are unaware of as by any abstract or long-division assessments our machines are capable of. We divide the world between the human and the nonhuman, leaving us as a miserable minority, shrinking the earth and ourselves with every passing day.

Ascension Day

WHILE WE WERE STILL SETTLING IN AND ADJUSTING TO our new land and its struggling trees, my heart still ached for what I had left behind in New Hampshire. I saw the lightning striking in the forestlands like the forked roots of a great tree. I walked past blue columbine and found painted trillium growing by the brook, with its bold and unfailing waters making their way down to the lake out of their source in the hill behind us. The little lavender flowers of the rhodora bloomed in spring on shrubs that lined the edge of the lake, with pink azalea overshadowed by the dark hemlocks behind them.

Beech trees with bark like blue and gray shadows from the sky grew on the upper slopes, from which we looked down onto the great white pines that lined the shores of the lake. They called me into their sweeping branches, where I built a tree house over the rock garden, an open platform from which I could feel their own measure of outer space. Dad once told me that he had built one as a boy in a tree down by the lake. Rudyard Kipling had been visiting his parents and had given the tree house an Indian name, which I now, alas, have forgotten.

In the spring clearings, the mating woodpeckers tapped out their semaphoric messages to each other on the trees. Before I owned a field guide to identify the birds, the veery, the wood thrush, and the hermit sang out from their own grounds on various levels. They now call to me, "You have been away. Where did you go?" I only had a rudimentary knowledge as a boy, but it did not matter. I was in on the beginning. Robert Frost, who lived in the hills of Vermont and New Hampshire, wrote, "Earth's the right place for love: I don't know where it's likely to go better."

For a number of years I taught classes in the newly established Environmental Studies Division at Dartmouth College, in Hanover, New Hampshire, during the fall term. I was a writer, not a trained professor, but the job was freer and more experimental than I might have expected, so it taught me as much as it did my students. I tried to turn their attention, as much as I could, to the out-of-doors, and one of my pleasures was to lead them on hiking trips during the weekends. I asked my fellow classmate at Harvard, Tudor Richards, an ornithologist and then director of the Audubon Society of New Hampshire, to join us on several occasions. I remember him telling us, on the way up one of the local mountains, that a 1000-foot elevation was roughly equivalent to 200 miles in latitude. With an increasing elevation and a lowering of the temperature there is a corresponding change in vegetation. All this has a direct effect on the distribution of nesting birds, each species with its own characteristics and subtle ways of living within its own habitat. There is an immense differentiation among birds that mirrors almost every region of the planet. They are regionalists, they are local identifiers, and they express the underlying complexities of a continent that we only approach from the surface. Merely identifying a species is never enough.

On a climb up Dartmouth's favorite home mountain, Mount Moosilauke, we met a little flock of boreal chickadees at a turn in the trail not far from the summit. They apparently spent much time in a black spruce bog that we passed on the way up. They shyly moved away as we came on, small brown versions of the black-capped chickadee that comes to our bird feeder and is tame enough to feed from our hands.

What you see at close range may capture a wilderness. The boreal chickadee ranges through coniferous forests from northern Labrador and Alaska south to northern New England, Ontario, Manitoba, and the state of Washington. According to my field guide, it nests not far from the ground. The nest is in some natural cavity and is constructed of moss, feathers, and "plant down." That was the only time I ever met a boreal chickadee, but its Indian wildness and rarity was worth climbing any height I was capable of. "Here I am," I thought, "in the presence of a real America we will not soon bury under our wheels." Yet we are in grave danger of starving it in our minds.

Some years later, when our summer home and the lands around it had been inherited by the U.S. Fish and Wildlife Service, I met David Anderson, a graduate of Antioch College, in Keene, New Hampshire, when he was being interviewed for a job with the Society for the Protection of New Hampshire Forests, in Concord. During my sporadic visits to my old home, he not only became a lasting friend, he also guided me toward the inner depths and details of a land I had once lived in without stopping to look at.

Dave, once from New Jersey, now lives in Sutton, not far from Newbury, where we lived. He and his wife made a commendable start, running the country store for a while. He has a sense for the right kind of roots to look for, like a porcupine or a skunk digging up grubs. Trees are in his nature, worth climbing, like the hilly heights above his house, and worth living with, like the black bear that makes a bed in the branches of a big beech tree, where it can feed on beechnuts. Dave and his wife live on a small farm, with fruit trees and chickens and their three kids, who have been encouraged to embrace natural living from the start. They have a wide area of priceless freshwater marsh just past their house, very rich in what modern society, in its remote association with nature, calls "wildlife," and that means a wealth of mosquitoes, which Dave welcomes as indispensable food for fish, ducks, and spring and summer songbirds, as well as frogs, all inheritors of that "web of life" that our world regularly invokes but seldom reveres.

Dave goes after detail with relish, building a case, on his field trips, for lives spent not in "going for the jugular," as he described a politician to me one day, but in seeing life straight, not as a bogus separation between human and nonhuman life, but as part of the great cosmic community of living things. He prefers the back roads, especially at night, when the headlights of his car pick up animal eyes along the way. He will also engage in a monologue of such untiring length as to make you think he has lost his way, but even if he has to bypass half a city, it is worth doing, because his method is circular, and he always comes back to where he started. Straight lines, he well knows, are deceiving. They only lead you to superficial elevations that you don't deserve. For him, life is full of local but not misleading stories. People don't know much if they can't recognize reality when they see it, even in the eyes of a coon, or in a crowd of young frogs in a wet meadow left by the beavers. You don't really learn much without making friends with what you meet.

It might seem to some that Dave is wasting time with inefficient meandering, but he is as wedded to universal sense as a pileated woodpecker or a noble tree hive of bees. The older I get, the more I learn from him, tagging behind on a long trail of humor and dedicated alliances.

One day we set out to climb up the back of Sunset Hill, which my grandfather had purchased in the late 1880s before building a house overlooking Lake Sunapee. We could see Lake Sunapee, named after *soonipee*, which means "wild geese," the name given to it by the original inhabitants. Its waters looked like a great silvery slash, and off toward the north the peaks of the Presidential Range were white with snow.

The trail started at the base of the hill in a grassy area at the edge of a small pond. It was in early May, as I remember it. We were at an elevation of about 800 feet. The temperature at night was still chilly, 20 to 40 degrees Fahrenheit, but the longer days had brought out the light spring green of young birches and poplars. We saw a woodcock secretively moving through the tall grasses by the pond, and a rose-breasted grosbeak was singing nearby. I have seldom heard more melodious high, flutelike notes. A common yellowthroat warbler was singing "witchety, witchety" by the shallow pond.

The local woods were full of other trails, now that the snow was gone. Some animals had left their tracks behind them, or some other slight evidence to give them away. Most, like the wildcat or the fisher, were nowhere to be seen. The black bear and the fox had crossed the trail, and the dark porcupine had found its black home at the base of a tree. Further up, we spotted other warblers, including the chestnut-sided and the black-throated green. Their calls are often hard to identify, sounding like buzzing insects through a tapestry of leaves, needles, and shaded branches. They travel from one place to another on breeding and mating flights before nesting. Like the leaves, they repopulate wooded and forested lands from the ground up. The warblers, called "rainbow birds" by the naturalist Edwin Way Teale, drift through canopies of leaves on all their varied levels. When breeding, the warblers are seldom noticed without patient attention, and their nests are hard to locate. "Who are we?" they sing, in their various travels through light and shadow everywhere. Distinctive behavior, appropriate to both humans and animals, can be seen in many bird families. We see courtship and aggression as we know it in ourselves, but many of these smaller travelers, who say no more than "zee-zee-zee," though more elusive are yet clear in their choices of distinctive ranges. They may be as yellow-green as a spring leaf, or, like the redstart or the blackburnian, a striking contrast of black and scarlet. We decorate the world because we think we own it, but they are its closest expression. How else can you really mate with light, the ascending and descending shadows across a hillside or a mountain slope?

I thought of the warbler wave now starting to move past us in the new light. They came in with transformations in the soil and in the spring awakening of countless plants and trees. It moved us, too, rising from winter's sleep. Early spring is not a natural phenomenon that needs interpretation; it moves in without thought. Yet the birds appear out of a wider affinity of place than we are aware of. The intellect may be a "cleaver," but it is unable to cut through all the intervening space and distance that are held in the minds of the birds. Their precision is astonishing. Their inner sense of the right place to nest over thousands of miles of hillsides and mountain slopes may be difficult for the rational mind to understand, but perhaps we have become too far removed from Earth's particulars to hold on; we may be adrift in all that space we call our own. A seabird such as a tern may come back to the same nest over an annual migration of thousands of miles. It is thought that individuals return to the places where they last heard a parent's voice. As Dave pointed out to me, the fidelity of nesting birds to their preferred habitats is even more specific when they are in breeding locales than when they are on migration.

I must confess that I never made it to the top of Sunset Hill that day. The way up had turned into a dry streambed full of big boulders that I found hard to navigate. We turned back in deference to my age. At the base of the hill we met an unpaved road, lined by a long stone wall and a barn of honorable age with weathered siding. We spotted a yellow-bellied sapsucker drilling holes in a sapling nearby. Above the barn the land was open to the sky. Once pasture, it lay across a wide green reach above the lower houses and roads leading toward town.

All this land, once under cultivation by a farming community, had been bought by a developer and was to be called High Meadow Estates. So, an age of tilling and slow time was to be replaced by real estate, access roads, cars, TV sets with their imaginary views, without a hand in the soil. Robert Frost wrote about people who were not so elevated, "You can't call it living, because it isn't."

During that earlier age, a panoramic view played second fiddle to a life of hard work spent holding "Mother Nature" down. The community prayed to an unforgiving God, and its members' lives were short and uncompromising. The idea of a heavenly kingdom was a relief from daily suffering and foreboding. Now, modern convenience has moved in, almost without effort. The new residents do not need to build stone walls and break their backs or dig the stubborn soil. Still, the dark green mountain slopes keep rolling northward with the clouds, and the migratory birds have moved in from distant tropical lands, or over whole seas to build their nests, each one in response to a center that never falls.

The Protection of Silence

IN 1914 MY FATHER BUILT A SMALL AND COMFORTABLE cottage on the shore of Lake Sunapee, 1000 feet above sea level, in anticipation of his marriage in 1915. Since the death of my parents, the cottage has been under the protection of the U.S. Fish and Wildlife Service and is maintained by a local group called the Friends of the John Hay Wildlife Refuge.

A narrow dirt road leads downhill to the hollow where the cottage lies, and it has always been bordered by splendid hemlocks and white pines that equaled the giant redwoods and sequoias when I was a boy and had never seen the west. The morning sun takes a long time to reach the small house because of the heights at its back. Dawn comes late, but when, after a few hours, the light comes flooding through the windows that face Mount Sunapee on the far side of the lake, the sun builds a shimmering roadway of molten gold between us and the mountain. As a boy, it filled me with confidence that slow time and all its protected travelers would never fail me.

In early spring, on the very edge of the shore where the lake waters move quietly in and around the rocks and the hemlocks hold the shade, the sweet-smelling flowers of the rhodora appear like little bells to meet the open light. The front door of the cottage faces the steep hill, and out of that hill came a spring of pure, cold water. A high stone wall still stands there, in fair condition (rock always lasts in New Hampshire), and at its center is a wooden, round-topped doorway, the entrance to a springhouse equipped with shelves to keep perishable food, such as fresh-caught fish from the lake, as well as milk, cream, and butter from our small family farm and its herd of Ayrshire cows.

One year, after my parents had died, I spent the night there. The door of the springhouse was old and warped and very hard to open. The cold water that once came in on both sides of the raised floor had been reduced to a trickle, but I listened and waited while all the intervening years streamed through my mind like mountain waters, imperishably new. The wall was thick with hanging and untended vines and as I stood there a tiny warbler skipped in and away, having touched down for a few seconds in time. It was a precious link with Latin America, a quick reminder of Dad's expeditions to the Yucatan. That little bird was like a flying light, vibrant with an unquenchable energy. The tribe of warblers had moved in like waves that touched on all the hills and mountains above us. They carried in the secrets of an uninvited cosmos, never subordinated to human use. To me, they were sacred visitors. My field guide could explain their range, their color, and general characteristics, but it was never enough to capture their irreplaceable nature. That which is not all mine steals in with the evening and wings away with the dawn.

The night began to be filled with the intense sound of motorboats, which went on long past nightfall; they seemed to have no purpose but getting from one end of the lake to the other in the fastest time. So, in a way, they were never there. Yet the bird and the seasons of my old home let me in. I joined all their live attachments and their secret being, within the high art of an inseparable attention. This manifold life, followed by the changing years, never stopped for strangers. Every life was measured by a greater burning, a higher, colder Arctic than we have the power to know. This measures us, and not the other way around. The warblers traveled on, like the flowers and the clouds, on their indispensable journey past denial or abuse.

When Clouds Take On a Life of Their Own

ONE LATE AFTERNOON IN MIDWINTER I WAS WALKING down our local beach, with nobody in sight at first, when I met two friends walking toward me. They told me to look for a rare sight ahead of me, out on the tides. It was almost high tide, and the sandbars offshore that form a limited barrier beach were beginning to disappear underwater, leaving what looked like the tops of small islands shining brightly in the sun. They were completely white, and when I turned my field glasses on them I could see that they were alive with birds. As each of those sandy patches disappeared under the rising tide, the birds burst into the air and flew along the shoreline.

These were the famous sand treaders and wave chasers that feed on crustaceans in the sand all along the coastline of Cape Cod. They sped by over the water in flocks that numbered at least several hundred individuals, though at that distance individuality disappeared. Some were dunlins, named for their dun-colored plumage, but their combined flights were white as snow. Hundreds of birds were transformed into single organisms flung across the surface of the water like undulating scarves made up of white beads glittering in the light. As if trying some reckless maneuver, a flock would suddenly curve back on itself, almost overturning, and then swing back with surprising resilience.

The far end of the beach is broken by a tidal channel bordered by a long rock jetty and a boat-building establishment on the opposite bank. At this point, the birds rose high in the air and hung above the shore like one giant bloom. Inside it, they were all spinning and circling together, held by some inner sense of their own. This self-propelled motion of theirs reminded me of the dark clouds of mosquitoes coming at dusk over the plains of Manitoba.

After a winter of feeding along coastal beaches, they would soon move on to their nesting grounds in the high Arctic. The species migrate along the polar belts of the earth, motivated by a far greater force than our own fits of "memory and desire." These belts must contain the outward pull of all the seas.

Down on the beach, held there by gravity and a weak constitution, I lost sight of them. The sun was sinking below the horizon. The receding waters along the scalloped shore were taking on the lambent, pearly colors of the nacre of a shell. The sky was turning a silvery gray, like the scales of a herring, while the water carried pink and blue reflections until the immemorial run of sunsets faded and was gone.

Those little sand dancers were shape changers, called into service by a timeless planet. It is this magical cohesion that holds the far ends of life together, past all the limits we impose on them.

The Bonds of Freedom

I LEARNED FROM WATCHING BIRDS OF THE SEA AND shore that each kind, whether it was a sanderling, an eider, a red-breasted merganser, or a loon, had its own dynamic relationship with the sea. They were not simply identified by looking up their names and characteristics in a field guide. Identification was one thing, and underlying complexities another. Each species had its own set of emotional and physical needs. Each played a distinct role in whatever part of the earth and sea it occupied. I did not know enough about any of them at first to describe them with much accuracy. Yet when I saw a bluebird on a February day it filled me with unfathomable delight.

I knew that if I only learned about facts and general characteristics in nature it would never be enough. I had been educated in nature's limitations, but the miracle of life, in no vague sense, lay in the supreme distinctions I began to see around me, from a leaf to a fly.

What moved those little sanderlings, wrapped in their own clouds, but a profound sense of geographical location from one end of the earth to the other? They shared in a magic common to all distinct forms of life from the depths of the sea to the heights of the sky. We could count as many species as we were able to. But it did not mean a great deal to compare life spans, as if men and elephants had some advantage over the insects. Common existence is the mystery. The flight of a gull, the metamorphosis of a butterfly—both are part of an everlasting engagement, denying death in the presence of immortal change.

I also began to see, after many years of trying to understand what I was looking at, that no life or season lacks ceremony. Over the years, we learned to watch for the arrival of the gannets, diving for fish out on the open waters of the bay. During the autumn months, they left their nesting colonies to the north and made their way past the shores of New England. We could spot them from the beach by the white bursts of spray they left behind them. They circled high in the air over the water and then plunged into the sea some fifty feet below them as they followed the schools of fish. They would fold their magnificent wings into great arrows as they dove below the surface. Local storms occasionally drove them closer to the shore with disastrous results. I have seen a few young ones, with black plumage as opposed to the white of adults, lying dead on the sand. Yet when storm winds forced them in, they usually mastered them with their six-foot wingspans and escaped disaster.

One summer we drove north to Quebec to see the gannetries in midseason at Bonaventure Island on the Gaspe Peninsula. The nests were crowded together on a strip of land high above the shining sea. Each nest contained large, gawky, half-grown chicks. There were hundreds of birds, always busy, and very noisy, but each pair of nesters guarded its own space and respected that of its near neighbor. We could take their pictures from only a few yards away, but we were warned not to stand too close. They had powerful beaks.

The young were being continuously fed by their parents, who shuttled back and forth between the cliff tops and the sea far below. I had never heard such an assembly of guttural communication in my life, and I could make no more sense of it at first than I did of the noisy white holland turkeys on my grandfather's farm. But the turkeys were scattered and undisciplined. When I met the wild gannets, on the other hand, a sense of pride and order held me fast.

One of the books I first consulted on animal behavior was by the British ornithologist Edward A. Armstrong. His *Bird Display and Behavior* begins with a chapter entitled "The Ceremonial of the Gannet":

> As we watch a gannet wheeling in the sky then plunging bodily into the sea we might think the bird a perfect symbol of unrestrained freedom. And yet a little investigation at close quarters shows us that its liberty is restricted in countless ways by what we may style the bonds of its own being and the conventions of a society. Like the apparently free and unrestrained behavior of the Australian aborigine, the gannet is dominated by a most rigid social system. It makes love and war ceremonially. There is a ritual of taking flight, of greeting, of nest building and of feeding a chick. All this would not be so unless in some measure ceremonial brought satisfaction and a sense of well being to the individual and propriety to the race.
>
> Man may learn of the gannet as well as of the ant, and human society would be happier if modern trends were less toward the organization of the insects and more toward the community life of the birds. Out of the

stresses in the individual as well as in society the gannet has evolved a variety of stately ceremonies which add interest and loveliness to life. Tension is the source of progress and the forcing ground of art and it is when individuals, of the society which they constitute, timorously and weakly abandon their duty to make this tension constructive that disaster ensues. (Edward A. Armstrong, *Bird Display and Behavior* [New York: Oxford University Press, 1947], 29.)

This book was written under the long shadow of the Great War of 1914, and to a contemporary reader who demands the immediate authority of science it may seem to lack heft. It is true that *Bird Display and Behavior* was published when the study of ecology and animal behavior were in their infancy. But what we might hear under Edward Armstrong's well-mannered style is a deep concern for what the war did to destroy a sense of humanity in our world.

Timing

THE FLOWER

One year, in the middle of a lifetime of trying to educate myself in the details of the natural world, I thought of flowers. I had been exposed to gardens for a long time, but I knew very little botany. Plants were either wild or tame, like the animals, and when I was young I just assumed that human cultivation was probably what motivated plants to do what they did. That a closer relationship with flowers might bring me nearer to what was missing in myself seldom occurred to me at first.

Then one day I noticed that a white California poppy I had planted from seed in our garden, along with the vegetables, was regularly opening and closing every morning and late afternoon. So I thought that perhaps I had wasted too much time seeing things from a distance. I had to get in there and watch. Therefore, I sat down next to one of those flowers at about four o'clock in the afternoon, when many other poppies had already closed up. Minutes passed before I really noticed much difference in that dish of petals spread out to take the light. Then I saw that it was definitely beginning to change. Motion was there, though barely perceptible. It was not mechanical, like a watch, but alive to the earth and sky, and therefore mysterious. The flower began to deepen and narrow into a cup. The stamens and pistils began to disappear at its base as the petals were closing in, settling and adjusting like the interfolded pages of a rolled newspaper. I suppose it took around three quarters of an hour before the process was completed. By then, I had become aware of a whole new cosmos, barely glimpsed, a new opening into time and space and into feeling. I had never thought of sense perception in a flower. But there it was, and I was beginning to move in at last. I am often faithless, like the rest of my race, but for a while after that experience I could not cut a new flower without wondering whether or not I had severed it too soon from its rightful universe. I had come a long way in a short time. As that night wore on, I was covered by a vast ceiling of stars, each one in the eye of a flower. Starflowers, every single one.

THE BOX TURTLE

Man's modern myth has us at the center of the universe, perhaps because it stems from a mind that we do not seem to be able to use very effectively in these reckless years. I would defer at this point to the turtle, who never knew how to conquer time but holds it within his shell.

I am not a real student of turtles, like David Carrol of New Hampshire, who can recognize a spotted turtle through long acquaintance as it floats in dark waters in the middle of the night. I have been a distant yet neighborly friend of turtles since I was a boy. I had not heard the myth that life began on the back of a turtle, but I was ready to believe it. I caught a wandering painted turtle on its out-of-water migration and innocently put it in a wire pen, where I fed it bread and water, effectively turning pen into prison. It died, as any responsible adult could have told me it would. All I could think of doing was to bury it under a big sugar maple that shaded the stone wall that ran across the back lawn.

Later on, I had a small collection of semiprecious stones, and in their shining they reminded me of turtles and their glossy backs. I have watched them absorbing solar radiation as they lined up together on a log out in the shallow waters of a pond. They seemed to have a faraway look in their eyes, which might suggest to some of us that they lacked intelligence. Clearly, they were not at all interested in our advanced methods of measuring time, or in our weightless conquest of it. They were parishioners of a home church deep within an enduring darkness, spotted by the sun.

When we first arrived on the Cape one of our new neighbors was a land turtle that slowly wandered through the scrub oaks and thickets with a strong territorial sense. When removed by summer tourists to the city, these turtles were hopelessly lost. They had been here for "time out of mind." One year a Cape Codder of the old school, who knew the nature of his land, picked up a box turtle whose shell had been inscribed by a deceased relative with his initials as well as the date, which was 1889, making the turtle seventy-one years old at the time. And it may have lived for many years after that, unless run over by a motorized vehicle with no sense of inner time at all.

It is now October of the year 2001. Slow time is no longer acceptable or understood. The box turtle population has declined since we were first aware of them. I suspect that they have survived up to now because they have kept pace with the trees, species of scrub oak and pitch pine that are now far higher than they used to be and that shade the turtles' progress. One afternoon, a visiting friend and I saw a box turtle in the woods by the side of our road. The leaves of the overhanging trees in the late fall had begun to change color. It was not the color of the maples that fire the mountain slopes to the north of us. The color of oaks, soon fading to brown, is more subdued, burnt orange, muted greens and yellows, fading red, but in the light of the October sun the leaves glittered and shook in the wind. They whirled and danced like birds and gradually drifted down to join a thick brown carpet of their forerunners on the ground. And there we saw one of the great survivors, with a wonderfully patterned shell of a brilliant deep gold like some ancient warrior helmet of the Bronze Age.

A few years ago, a fire broke out in the woods behind our house. It was put out by a number of trucks from neighboring towns. I suspected that dirt bikes might have been the cause, since I had seen scorched areas in dry lichen-covered slopes across our property. A few days after the fire was out we walked across the area with Mark Robinson, the conservationist, and found a wide circle of scorched, sandy ground and a few blackened pines. At the very center was a lone box turtle that did not move as we came on, as if it had been disoriented. His small red eyes shone like burning coals in the desert. We picked him up and moved him to the fallen leaves he was accustomed to, and he was on his long life's journey again. The fires human beings set are worldwide, but the turtle is still at a center that will outlast us.

Freedom of the Seas

CAPE COD HAS ALWAYS HAD A TRANSITORY NATURE. Whatever we have done to consciously change and bury it, or to make money and move on, it belongs to the sea itself. Man finds himself in the unhappy and often desperate position of not being able to turn back the tides, or his own growing avalanche of unsettlement on a shrinking land.

The sea will ultimately bury the Cape. Sea levels are rising, due to the melting of the ice caps around the poles. It is estimated that the island of Nantucket will disappear beneath the waves in some 900 years, and the Cape will eventually follow. So the high bluffs along the outer beach facing the Atlantic will continually return their sands to the sea.

On a stormy day, when the wind was blowing furiously from the northeast, I was standing on top of the cliff at

Nauset Beach when I suddenly became aware that a great crack was starting to widen not more than 20 feet ahead of me. It was almost like looking down into lava beds on the shores of Iceland and getting a glimpse of those everlasting fires under the earth's surface, like the pits of Dante's Inferno.

I can always count on the seabirds that fly in or migrate offshore, almost all the year round, to give me better guidance to where I live. They pull me out from where I am, as the moon harnesses the tides, and the great sea winds blow in to tell us where all real distance can be found.

Seasonal voices also tell me where I am. Robins in winter guide me to where last year's fruits and berries can be found. During early spring, the reedy, flutelike "ok-a-lee" of the redwings rises out of the rushes in the marsh. One evening, when the setting sun produced a great band of molten gold along the horizon, I watched a flock of redwings lift out of their nesting sites to meet it. I have also seen terns, nesting on a rocky island in the sea many miles from shore, leave their nesting sites in the bare ground and then return to them as if in homage to the sun. No life lacks ceremony. The real truth in nature lies in the eye of a bird, the veins of a leaf, the transformation of a butterfly. We can never fix them in our minds as if we could control inner time as well or better than they do.

It is now October, toward the end of the month, late morning. From the beach overlooking the bay, I watch the sea moving out calmly and majestically, with hardly a breath of wind to ruffle its surface. Long flights of eiders follow the coastline. An irregular flock of wintering brant geese cross the bay, and I see a small flock of them hover high in the sky, dark and thin, shaped like a question mark. Inshore, a mixed flock of herring and ring-billed gulls rides in the shallow, protected waters of a long rock jetty that stretches out from the beach. A little golden plover perches on the rock. A few yellowlegs fly in to follow the curving sands of the inlet past the jetty. Suddenly, out of some unseen motivation, all the gulls fly up crying and move further down the shoreline, sending the plover with them. But miles away, toward the shores of Wellfleet and Truro, I get a glimpse, through my field glasses, of the gannets. There might be a hundred of them. The light of the morning sun shines on their white wings as they pitch down, one after another, into the sea following a school of fish. Their energy seems incredible; it takes my breath away. Their beautifully precise and rhythmic abandon, part of a repeated lifelong circling and hovering and moving on, symbolizes the tireless heights and depths of nature.

In flight, seabirds carry Earth's distances in their own passion for being. They lift up and travel on ahead of us as they have done for thousands of years. Mechanical flight is only blind and cumbersome by comparison. I followed the terns I first learned to recognize on the Cape all the way overseas to Laeso, an island north of Jutland, and from there to the coast of England. Here, they come in again, with their sharply etched bodies and forked tails, "sea swallows," hirondelle de mer, diving for small fish as they go, in their own splendid style. Their ritualistic flights in courtship are surpassingly elegant. I see nothing in our lives that is any better. They followed the mysteries long before we appropriated them as our own.

I would like to stay here a little longer now, waiting for more messengers from the gods.

Library of Congress Cataloging-in-Publication Data

Hay, John, 1915–

Mind the gap : the education of a nature writer /
John Hay.

p. cm. — (Environmental arts and humanities series)

ISBN 0-87417-595-X (alk. paper)

1. Hay, John, 1915– 2. Poets, American—20th century—
Biography. 3. Naturalists—United States—Biography. 4.
Natural history—United States. 5. Outdoor life—United
States. 6. Natural history—Authorship. I. Title. II. Series.

PS3558.A828Z47 2004

813'.54—dc22 2004006184